Harry J. Wilmot-Buxton

German, Flemish and Dutch Painting

Harry J. Wilmot-Buxton

German, Flemish and Dutch Painting

ISBN/EAN: 9783337300951

Printed in Europe, USA, Canada, Australia, Japan

Cover: Foto ©Thomas Meinert / pixelio.de

More available books at **www.hansebooks.com**

ILLUSTRATED TEXT-BOOKS OF ART, EDITED
BY EDWARD J. POYNTER, R.A.

GERMAN, FLEMISH

AND

DUTCH PAINTING

BY H. J. WILMOT-BUXTON, M.A.,

AND

EDWARD J. POYNTER, R.A.

LONDON
SAMPSON LOW, MARSTON, SEARLE & RIVINGTON
Limited
St. Dunstan's House
FETTER LANE, FLEET STREET, E.C.
1890

PREFACE.

THE painters of Germany and the Netherlands provide for the English Art-Student a field of study no less interesting than that furnished by the celebrated Italian Masters.

In Germany—after a school of painters who worked with a deep and honest purpose but with no immense genius—Art, in the persons of Dürer and Holbein, made an advance of incomparable importance ; and owing to the fact that Holbein spent many of his best years in England, and here painted a large number of his finest works, we have an additional reason for a careful study of the great German Renaissance.

After these masters and their immediate disciples, Art gradually declined in the hands of such copyists as Mengs who was nothing better than a feeble imitator of Michelangelo, and of Denner who smothered Art by his excessive elaboration. The later revival under Cornelius and Overbeck, if it does not arouse enthusiasm, at least commands respect and admiration.

The early schools of Holland and Flanders were so closely allied that it is difficult to divide their honours. To the Van Eycks of Bruges is due the discovery of an improved method of using oil as a vehicle in painting, and they and their followers have never been surpassed in technical excellence.

Then followed Matsys and the early school of Antwerp, and after him came the decline, hastened by over-wrought composition and a futile straining after the style of the Italians. This decline was happily checked by the advent of Rubens, the Titian of the North, whose Art is manly, although it does not possess the idealism or religious sentiment of Italy, or even of the early Flemings.

With his greatest pupil, Van Dyck, all Englishmen are familiar. and indeed this country has an almost equal claim with Flanders to rank him among her painters.

We trace a gradual decline through Snyders, Jordaens, and other pupils of Rubens—through Teniers, Lely, and others of less note, and Art had almost died out, when it again awoke to new life under Henri Leys and his celebrated school.

The very early Dutch painters were almost Flemish in character, and it was not until the time of Rembrandt that Holland could be said to possess a school of her own.

Rembrandt formed many artists of the first rank; and his influence for good was felt in his country longer perhaps than that of any other individual master. With him and his followers began the realisation of the ideal of Dutch Art—the representation of the people and their doings. The painters of Holland who stayed at home and depicted what they saw in their own land, produced works of far greater interest than their fellow countrymen who went to Italy and strove in vain to rival the artists of the South.

The principal pupils of Rembrandt were Gerard Dou, Ferdinand Bol, Govaert Flinck, Carel Fabritius, and Nicolaas Maas. In Dou, Bol and Flinck, we find artists who produced works of most minute finish without loss of breadth in composition and execution; and in De Hooch and Ver Meer, masters almost unequalled in their treatment of light—a legacy which they had received from Rembrandt.

It is to Holland also that we turn for the greatest masters of landscape, architecture, animal and marine painting—Hobbema, Ruisdael, Cuyp, Potter, Van de Velde, and Bakhuisen; and even when they descended to such trivialities as the flowers of Van Huysum, the fowls of D'Hondecoeter, or the kitchens of Kalf, the paintings of Holland are still of absorbing interest.

English noblemen were the first to recognise and appreciate the merits of several of these artists, and this country possesses (as the recent exhibitions of Old Masters at Burlington House have shown) more of the *chefs-d'œuvre* of Dutch painters than Holland herself.

To every thoughtful English reader the history of Art in Germany and the Netherlands should be a subject of great interest.

H. J. W. B.

April, 1881.

CONTENTS.

BOOK II.—PAINTING IN FLANDERS.

BOOK. III.—PAINTING IN HOLLAND.

LIST OF ILLUSTRATIONS.

GFDP *b*

PAINTING IN GERMANY.

NOTE.

THROUGHOUT the book the names of the painters as they signed their canvases are always given first, but in the text they are spoken of under the names by which they are generally known.

When the names have been habitually printed wrong—as Terburg for Ter Borch, Vandyke for Van Dyck, or Breughel for Brueghel—it has been thought better to give them in their correct form only.

The letters *ij* in Dutch and Flemish are equivalent to the letter *y* pronounced long. Thus Eyck might be written Eijck, Dyck, Dijck, and Massys similarly in the old text is Massijs; and the name of the famous Dutch cattle-painter is written by himself Cuijp.

GERMAN, FLEMISH AND DUTCH PAINTING.

INTRODUCTION.

ART in Germany and the Netherlands owes its origin to Christianity as interpreted by the Byzantines. At first Art was repudiated by the Christians as savouring of idolatry; gradually, however, it became the handmaid of Religion and the teacher of divine truths.

Beginning with symbols of Our Saviour and His Passion, the early Christian painters went on to illustrate their faith by wall-pictures, such as decorate the Catacombs of Rome and Naples, the earliest-known specimens of Christian painting. But these artists had been, as a rule, painters first and Christians afterwards, and the influence of Classic or Pagan Art remained. This is very observable in the pictures of the Catacombs, where Christ is frequently depicted as Orpheus taming the wild animals with the music of his lyre. The Art of Byzantium, on the other hand, rejected utterly the

Classic ideal in its treatment of sacred subjects. The ancient Greek had delighted to paint the beauties of the human form in pictures of sensuous loveliness. The monks of Byzantium treated the subjects of their Art with the sternest asceticism, endeavouring to teach the subjection of the flesh to the spirit. Shut out from the world, which was in a state of transition, "the old order changing, and giving place to new," these monks laboured at a form of Art which never advanced, but in time took the place of the Classical Christian school, which entirely disappears from the later paintings in the Catacombs.

It was doubtless from the quiet monasteries of these Byzantine monks that Art, in the form of illuminated manuscripts, was first introduced to the rude inhabitants of Northern Europe.

We find no trace of painting in Germany or the Netherlands before the introduction of Christianity. Charlemagne, the patron of knowledge, the friend of Alcuin and Eginhard, would have been also a patron of the Arts had his military expeditions allowed him sufficient leisure. As it was, he beautified the Cathedral of Aachen (Aix-la-Chapelle) with mosaics, and his own palace with wall-pictures. The remains of a mosaic in the cupola of the Cathedral have been discovered under a coating of whitewash, where Christ is represented throned in glory, and the four-and-twenty elders holding their golden crowns. In addition to the Cathedral of Aachen and the Palace of Charlemagne, the Castle of Upper Ingelheim, on the Rhine, was adorned with frescoes— those in the chapel illustrating scenes from the Bible, those in the banqueting halls dealing with battle-pieces. There the deeds of Cyrus and Hannibal, Alexander and Romulus, were contrasted with those of Charles Martel, of Pepin and Charlemagne himself. No signs of these pictures remain to us, but we learn from miniatures of them that the sacred subjects bear traces of Byzantine influence. This influence is also very remarkable in the manuscripts which are still extant. For example, in an Evangeliarium at Paris we find a figure of Christ giving the Benediction in the form used in the Byzantine Church. In an Evangelistarium preserved in the Town Library of Trèves we can trace another influence besides that of Byzantium. The monks who, in the sixth century, inhabited the Irish monasteries were very skilful in a special form of illumination. Such men as St. Columbanus, St. Gallus, St. Kilian, St. Lievin, and St. Willebrord visited various parts of Europe in their missionary travels, and took their Art with them. This Irish influence is very plainly visible in the Manuscript of Trèves.

Among the specimens of early German Art we may mention some pen drawings still extant. They may be found in the miniatures of a manuscript now in the Munich Library bearing the date 814, and belonging to the Convent of Wessobrunn in Bavaria. The illumination of manuscripts was the favourite style of Art in Germany at this early period, and is the only form in which it has been preserved to us. By degrees the German clergy even of the highest rank cultivated this kind of painting, and during the prosperous epoch extending from 919 to 1066 we find glimpses of originality, though the influence of Byzantine teaching is very clear. The middle of the eleventh century is marked by a stagnation in German Art, and no progress can be seen till the beginning of the following century. We find at this period mere outlines filled up with illumination of a slender kind, where the antique is but as a shadow of the past, and the robust originality of the future is yet to come.

From 1150 to 1250 Art in Germany and the Netherlands became endowed with new and vigorous life. The monasteries ceased to be the sole repositories of painting, and Art, once free from the narrowing influence of the convent, developed into a wider and healthier condition. Sacred subjects now took a wider range, and the legends of heroes, the stories of Charlemagne and Arthur, and the graceful traditions of the Niebelungen furnished themes for the painter. We get the figures, dresses, and arms of living men and women, drawn from the life, in place of the stiff, uniform, and unlovely shapes which Byzantine art delighted to perpetuate. Still the influence of this school is very prominent in the ecclesiastical pictures of this period, especially in paintings of the Crucifixion. In the nuns' choir in the Cathedral of Gurk in Carinthia is a wall-painting (Fig. 1) said to be of this period, which shows considerable advancement. It represents the *Virgin with the Holy Child in her arms*, seated on a throne supported by Solomon's lions. In the spandrels beneath are figures of two bishops—one of whom did not live to wear the mitre, which is, consequently, placed at his side.

In the miniatures in manuscripts we find a new element introduced—that of every-day life. A favourite subject is the description of the Months, with the work of the sower, the reaper, and the vine-dresser. The wall-pictures of Germany which remain to us from this age are rare: they show a decided advance in originality, though coarse in outline, with faint lights and shadows. In the Netherlands

FIG. 1.—MADONNA AND CHILD.   ABOUT 1214.
From a wall-painting in the Cathedral of Gurk in Carinthia.

the progress of Art kept pace with that of Germany, but the
Byzantine influence is stronger, probably because the Counts
of Flanders under the Latin Empire held the throne of
Constantinople.   Wall-paintings were, from the testimony
of Wolfram von Eschenbach, general at this time, but no
specimens have been preserved.

FIG. 2.—WALL-PAINTING.   EARLY 14TH CENTURY.

In the Chapel at Ramersdorf, near Bonn.

BOOK I.

THE GERMAN SCHOOLS.

CHAPTER I.

THE ORIGIN OF THE GERMAN SCHOOL.
[1350—1450.]

THE period of Art History which we have to consider in this volume commences with the latter years of the fourteenth century. If we fix on the year 1350 as a stand-point, we can take a rapid glance at the lights and shadows of four centuries. Looking back from this stand-point, we see Art rising in a glorious resurrection under the influence of Christianity, and mainly dedicated to the decoration of holy things and holy places. Looking forward from the same stand-point, we shall see the world, though growing old, endowed with a new and vigorous youth. We shall see the unlovely clouds of ignorance, superstition, and tyranny, which enveloped the Middle Ages, melting away; and the light of a clearer and better time, which was to guide men to

new worlds and new discoveries, rising into brightness. We
shall see the favourite dream of the Middle Ages, the dream of
a world-wide Church and world-wide dominion, embodied in the
Holy Roman empire, vanishing away. We shall see a revival of
learning, which produces a spirit of inquiry and speculation, and
an originality of idea which will find its exponent in Art. Still
looking forward, we shall see a vast Revolution, religious as well
as political, affecting the greater part of Europe, and exercising a
marked influence upon the history of Art. Unquestioning obedi-
ence henceforth gives place to a spirit of freedom, and Art, ceasing
to be exclusively the handmaid of religion, becomes the delineator
· of everyday life. We shall see Art in Germany flourishing in the
most glorious period of German history, and then disappearing
under the blight of that terrible war of thirty years, when men's
hearts were failing them, and unwarlike hands were forced to
leave the graver or the brush and seize the sword. Still looking
forward, we shall see Art in Holland dawning with the dawn
of liberty, and expressing with a bold, yet simple freedom, the
feelings of a bold, a free, and a simple people.

The German School produced nothing worthy of note for a
century after the Italian Schools of Florence and Siena had
emancipated themselves from Byzantine tradition, and we must
look for its origin in

THE SCHOOL OF BOHEMIA.
[1348—1378.]

This School arose and flourished under the fostering hand of the
Emperor Charles IV., although there had been an earlier dawn of
Art in Bohemia. Of the men of this School, and of their work,
we know very little. All that we do know is, that Charles IV.
employed several artists to adorn the walls of the church and
castle of Karlstein, near Prague; and that among them were
three men of note—THEODORICH, of Prague, NICOLAUS WURMSER,

and KUNZ. Their pictures are wall-paintings, now almost obliter-
ated, and no one can even tell us the special work of each of
these obscure masters. To Theodorich of Prague are attributed
one hundred and twenty-five figures of *Saints and Holy Men* in
the chapel of Karlstein. Nicolaus Wurmser is credited with
several scenes from the *Apocalypse*, on the walls of the same
chapel, and a *Crucifixion*, in the Imperial Gallery of Vienna, is
also attributed to him. Kunz is said to have painted scenes
from the life of his patron, Charles IV., in the church of Our
Lady. Another of the Emperor's clients was TOMMASO DA
MODENA, who beautified the chapel of St. Catherine, and who
belongs, strictly speaking, to the Italian School

The early Art of Germany, like that of Italy, was based upon
the model of the Byzantine, and the chief point of interest in the
School of Bohemia is the gradual upward striving from slavery
towards freedom and originality.

The School of Nuremberg was a school of sculpture, but we
find some paintings; the Imhof altar-piece is famous; it was
painted about the year 1420; its author is unknown, but its
execution proves it to be the work of no mean artist.

THE SCHOOL OF COLOGNE
[1358—1556.]

Foremost among these early Schools of German art stands the
School of Cologne. Whilst the Bohemian School was destined
to die away after a brief existence, that of Cologne became the
parent of two famous branches which stretched out to the east
and west of the Rhine—the Schools of Germany and of the
Netherlands. The city of Cologne was specially fitted by its
situation and character as the birth-place of Art. It was first
among the cities of Germany, even from the days of Charlemagne,
and it was one of the first northern towns to catch the influence
of the wandering painter from Italian or Byzantine Schools. Very

shadowy are the figures of the painters of the early School of Cologne.

We know of WILHELM of HERLE, commonly called MEISTER WILHELM, who, according to the 'Limburg Chronicle,' "was a famous painter in Cologne, whose equal was not to be found in Christendom; and who painted a man as though he lived." All we can know of Meister Wilhelm's life is, that he was born in the small village of Herle, near Cologne; that from 1358 to 1372 he lived and painted in Cologne; that he died about 1378, and that his works live after him. The chief painting attributed to him is the *Life of Christ*, now in the Johannis Kapelle in Cologne Cathedral. The *Scenes from the Life of Christ and the Virgin*, and *The Madonna and Child adored by Saints*, on an altar-piece, both in the Berlin Museum, were formerly ascribed to Meister Wilhelm, but are now classed as of his school. The National Gallery has a picture of *Sancta Veronica* from this master's hand.

STEPHAN LOCHNER, or MEISTER STEPHAN, who was possibly a pupil of Meister Wilhelm, has achieved greater fame than his teacher. Probably, however, the idea of Stephan having studied under the care of Wilhelm is a mistake. This we know of him for certain, that he was born at Constance, when we know not; but he was in Cologne in 1442, and had a house there of his own. In 1448 he represented the Guild of St. Luke in the town of his adoption, as a member of the Senate; again in 1451 he occupied the same post of honour, but died poor and uncared for in the same year. These few fragments of biography are gathered from some old registers, where Herr Merlo found the name of Stephan Lochner, or Loethener. There is an entry in the journal of Albrecht Dürer, which first made known the claims of Meister Stephan to the praise of critics; it tells us in the words of the great master: "Item, I have paid two silver pennies to have opened the picture which Meister Stephan painted at Cologne." And this same picture is the famous altar-piece in

FIG. 3.—MADONNA IN THE ROSE-ARBOUR. BY MEISTER STEPHAN.
In the Cologne Museum.

Cologne Cathedral, known as the " dom-bild," always attributed
to Meister Wilhelm before this statement of Dürer's.   The
" dom-bild," which has been been favourably compared with the
master-pieces of the Van Eycks, is a triptych; on the outside
there is an *Annunciation*, and within an *Adoration of the Magi;*
on one wing appear *St. Gereon and his knights*, on the other *St.
Ursula and her virgins.*   The figures are all painted on a gold
background, and the green foreground with its many flowers
seems to anticipate the rich colours of the oil-painters of Flanders.
Another grand work of this master is *The Madonna in the Rose-
Arbour* (*Madonna in der Rosenlaube*) in the Cologne Museum
(Fig. 3).

MEISTER CHRISTOPHORUS—known also as the "Master of the
Cologne Crucifixion," and the "Master of the Bartholomäus Altar"
—flourished in Cologne between 1500 and 1510.   His chief works,
which, like all those of his school, are devotional, represent the *In-
credulity of St. Thomas* (1501); the *Crucifixion*, formerly in the
Rathhaus of Cologne; and seven saints from an altar-piece, five
of which are in the Munich and two in the National Gallery.

In connection with this school we must mention the MASTER
OF THE DEATH OF THE VIRGIN; the picture from which he derives
his name, bearing the date 1515, is in the Museum of Cologne.
He found a pupil in BARTHOLOMÄUS BRUYN, who having shown
vigour and originality in his youth, fell into the prevailing error
of copying the Italians.   He died at Cologne in 1556.

From the School of Cologne sprang, as we have said,
two vigorous branches on the two banks of the Rhine, which
developed into the Schools of Germany and Flanders; and before
the end of the fifteenth century the School of Flanders was the
teacher of the Germans.   ROGIER VAN DER WEYDEN, a Fleming,
was the favourite master in the German School of this time,
and had supplanted Meister Stephan.

In the School of Westphalia we find two nameless Masters,
one the MASTER OF THE LYVERSBERG PASSION (about 1463—

1480), and the MASTER OF LIESBORN. The former clearly shows the Flemish influence in his style. His name is unknown, though he was formerly confounded by mistake with the engraver, Israel von Meckenen. The masterpiece which gives him his title is called the *Lyversberg Passion*, which belonged at one time to Herr Lyversberg. It is in eight compartments, representing the Passion of our Lord, and though not so noble and lofty in idea as some of the works of the Masters of Cologne, it displays greater knowledge of form and the art of colour.

The MASTER OF LIESBORN painted in the Benedictine Abbey of Liesborn sometime about 1465 ; and two parts of his great altar-piece are in our National Gallery. The chief part of this work was cut to pieces by Vandal hands when the convent was suppressed in 1807.

CHAPTER II.

THE GERMAN SCHOOL.

THE PRECURSORS OF ALBRECHT DÜRER.

(1420—1520.)

PASSING from the shadowy names and half-obliterated works of these early schools, we stay for a moment on the very brink of that Reformation which was to do so much both of good and evil for Religion and for Art, to recall some Masters who, though living before Luther, and still under the discipline of the Roman Church, yet began to think for themselves, and to give signs of that new era of art of which Albrecht Dürer and Holbein are the exponents.

MARTIN SCHONGAUER, more generally known as MARTIN SCHÖN, or "der hübsche Martin"—the "Bel Martino" of the Italians, and the "Beau Martin" of France—so named from the beauty of his works, was born probably at Colmar about 1450. He was the greatest painter Germany produced in the fifteenth century, and has been claimed as a native by both Augsburg and Ulm. Whilst going to the Flemish School for his colour, Schongauer preserved his originality and is thoroughly German in his works.

He commenced life as a goldsmith and an engraver—the favourite crafts of his age—and afterwards became a painter. We can trace the hard, delicate hand of the engraver amidst the brilliant colouring of his pictures, which are very rare. His chief works, or at least the chief works attributed to him, are a *Virgin and Child*, forming an altar-piece, at St. Martin's Church in Colmar, where the Virgin is surrounded by a bower of blooming roses; *St. Anthony*, in the Museum at Colmar (Fig. 4); and the *Death of the Virgin*, now in the National Gallery, the authenticity of which is, however, very doubtful. Schongauer is more famous as an engraver than a painter; there is a valuable collection of his prints in the British Museum, where the marvellously beautiful rendering of his female figures proves his right to the title of "Beau Martin." But apart from the beauty of his figures, we find a weird, unearthly, almost grotesque, spirit in some of his works which was quite unknown to the strict painters of religious art before the Reformation. The Church of Rome, as it allowed no deviation from its faith, seems to have forced its painters into a stereotyped treatment of sacred subjects, and it is only with the new thoughts and new life of the Reformation period, that we find a deviation from this rule. The weird, wild fancies of the German legends began to appear embodied in art, and of this revolution Schongauer was the pioneer. The print of *St. Anthony tormented by Demons* fully expresses the fantastic side of Schongauer's genius. This master died at Colmar, in 1488.

To the same school of Swabia belongs BARTHOLOMÄUS ZEITBLOM, a disciple of Schongauer. Neither the date of his birth nor that of his death is known. He flourished in Ulm and the neighbourhood, from about 1484 to 1516. Many of his pictures adorn churches in Swabia, but the best collection of his works is in the gallery of Stuttgardt. We cannot find in his pictures any trace of the new ideas which are to be seen in his Master's works.

To the same school belongs MARTIN SCHAFFNER, who flourished

FIG. 4.—ST. ANTHONY. BY SCHONGAUER.
In the Museum at Colmar.

FIG. 5.—ST. ANTHONY. BY GRÜNEWALD
In the Museum at Colmar.

from about 1499 to 1535 in Ulm, and who, like so many others, forsook the paths of original German thought for slavish imitation of the Italians.

The early School of Franconia was represented by MICHAEL WOLGEMUT,* a native of Nuremberg (born 1434, died 1519), who devoted himself chiefly to the carving and manufacture of huge altar-chests and other specimens of church furniture. All his pictures show clearness in colouring, and are not wanting in power; but they are very unequal. In his earlier years he produced four pictures representing scenes from the *Passion*, now in the Munich Gallery. A later work, painted in 1479, is a large altar-piece at Zwickau, which shows a marked improvement upon his earlier productions (Fig. 6). Some single figures of saints, now in the chapel of St. Maurice at Nuremberg, are still more favourable specimens of Wolgemut's style.

MATTHIUS GRÜNEWALD, born probably at Frankfort about 1460, was one of the best German painters of his time, and was clearly a pupil of both the Schools of Swabia and Franconia. He was favoured by the patronage of Albrecht, Archbishop of Mayence. His chief work is an altar-piece of six panels, now in the Gallery of Munich; it depicts the *Conversion of St. Maurice by St. Erasmus:* on the side-pieces are *St. Lazarus,* the *Magdalen, St. Martha,* and *St. Chrysostom.* In the Museum of Colmar there is a picture of *St. Anthony* by him (Fig. 5). Grünewald worked principally at Mayence and Aschaffenburg, and died after 1529 at Frankfort.

And now we find ourselves in the midst of the life which the storm of the Reformation created—a new life in Art no less than in Religion. Men no longer looked back, and dwelt with dreamy eyes on the forms and fancies of the past; now their eyes were strained eagerly forward to see the light of a new knowledge. The invention of printing, the discovery of America, the revival

* Sometimes written Wohlgemuth.

of learning, all combined to call men's thoughts from the dead
past to the living present.   Art in Italy went back to Pagan
Greece and Rome, but Art in Germany went forward under these
influences, and became the expression of the National character,
under its greatest Master, Albrecht Dürer.

Fig. 6.—The Birth of Christ. By Wolgemut.
Part of an altar-piece in the Marienkirche at Zwickau.

CHAPTER III.

ALBRECHT DÜRER AND HIS FOLLOWERS.
(1471—1550).

THE School of Franconia, and the studio or workshop of Michael Wolgemut, possess the honour of having given to the world the greatest Master of German Art.

ALBRECHT DÜRER was born in Nuremberg, on the 21st of May, 1471. As we look upon the portrait of the Master, painted by himself (Fig. 7), we seem to see the grey old town of Nuremberg, which from many causes has been made famous, and which has gained an undying lustre reflected from Albrecht Dürer. Gazing on the portrait of the great Master, and thinking of the old town, we are tempted to quote the lines of the American poet who sings to us so sweetly how,—

"In the valley of the Pegnitz, where across broad meadow-lands
  Rise the blue Franconian Mountains, Nuremberg, the ancient, stands.
      *   *   *   *   *   *   *
  Here, when Art was still religion, with a simple, reverent heart,
  Lived and laboured Albrecht Dürer, the Evangelist of Art ;
  Hence in silence and in sorrow, toiling still with busy hand,
  Like an emigrant he wandered, seeking for the Better Land.
  Emigravit is the inscription on the tomb-stone where he lies ;
  Dead he is not—but departed—for the artist never dies."

What do we know of his life?   His father was a Hungarian,
who settled in Nuremberg as a goldsmith.   Albrecht Dürer was
taught his father's trade, but fortunately his talent for art was
observed, and he was sent, in 1484, a boy of thirteen years, to
Schongauer.   This has been disputed, but there seems little
doubt of its truth.   In 1486 he was apprenticed to Michael
Wolgemut for three years.   From the studio of his master,
Albrecht Dürer passed, in the year 1490, to a new world—he
travelled; and in those "wander-years," which lasted till 1494,
he was doubtless laying in stores of learning for the after-time ;
but unfortunately we know nothing of those years, except that
he had a glimpse of Venice, the first sight of the Italian paradise
which, in his case, though seen again, never made him unfaithful
to the art of his fatherland.   In 1494, Albrecht Dürer returned
to Nuremberg, and married Agnes Frey, the daughter of a singer.
He received two hundred florins with his wife for her dowry, and
it has been said that with her he found more than two thousand
unhappy days.   Dürer's intimate friend, Willibald Pirkheimer, to
whom he seems to have confided most of his joys and sorrows,
has described Agnes Frey as a shrew, with a bitter tongue, and a
miserly spirit, who worried her husband to a premature death.
Apologists have been found for Agnes Frey in late years, but it
is now the fashion to whiten characters hitherto considered black,
and Agnes Frey may as well find an advocate as Richard III.
or Henry VIII.

In 1506, Dürer again travelled to Italy, and found a warm
welcome from the painters of Venice, a city which he now be-
held for the second time.   Doubtless he learned much from the
works which he saw, and the criticism which he heard, but,
fortunately for his country, he could go to Italy without becoming
a copyist.   Giovanni Bellini paid him especial honour, and Dürer
tells us that he considered Bellini "the best painter of them
all."   The great Master must have felt thus early that he was
almost "without honour" in his own city.   Nuremberg did not

FIG. 7.—PORTRAIT OF ALBRECHT DÜRER. BY HIMSELF.
In the Pinakothek at Munich.

appreciate its greatest son. We find Dürer writing to his dear
friend and gossip, Pirkheimer, to whom he often, doubtless,
confided the miseries of his home-life, his feelings and experiences
in Venice.   He tells him that in Venice he meets with "many
pleasant companions, so that it does one's heart good to be with
them; learned men, and lute-players, pipers, connoisseurs in art—
all very noble-minded, upright, virtuous people, who bestow on
me much honour and friendship." *Here*, he says, he is a
gentleman, but at home a parasite. " How I shall freeze after
this sunshine ! "   Still in a year he was again in Nuremberg,
and was patiently doing his work in spite of the coldness of his
townsfolk, and the tongue of his wife ; having refused an offer
of two hundred ducats a year, which the Venetian government
had made to induce him to remain among them.   Between the
years 1507 and 1520, Dürer produced many of his most famous
works.   In 1509, he bought a house for himself in the Zisselgasse
at Nuremberg.   In 1515, Raphael sent a sketch from his own
pencil to his great brother, who has been well styled the "Raphael
of Germany." The sketch is in red chalk, and is preserved in the
collection of the Archduke Charles at Vienna ; it bears this
inscription written by Dürer himself : " 1515, Raphael of Urbino,
who has been so highly esteemed by the Pope, drew these naked
figures, and sent them to Albrecht Dürer in Nuremberg, to show
him his hand."   In 1520, we find Dürer appointed court-painter
to the emperor Charles V., a position which he had already held
under Maximilian.   His own countrymen seemed to have been
niggardly in their reward of genius, for the court-painter had
only a salary of one hundred florins a-year, and painted portraits
for a florin (about twenty English pence).   In the same year
Dürer, accompanied by his wife, visited the Netherlands; and at
Antwerp, then the most important town of the Low Countries,
both he and his wife were entertained at a grand supper ; the
master has recorded in his journal his pleasure at the honour
bestowed upon him.   At Ghent and Bruges all were delighted

to show their respect for his genius. At Brussels, Dürer was summoned to the court of Margaret of Austria, Regent of the Netherlands, to whom he presented several engravings. Either through jealous intrigues, or from some other cause, his court favour was of short duration. In Brussels he painted several portraits which were never paid for, and for a time he was in straitened circumstances. Just at this time, however, Christian II., king of Denmark, became acquainted with him, and having shown every mark of honour to the painter, sat to him for his portrait. Soon afterwards he returned to Germany.

Once more at home in his beloved Nuremberg, Dürer wrote to remind the Town Council that whilst the people of Venice and Antwerp had offered him liberal sums to dwell among them, his own city had not given him five hundred florins for thirty years of work. But we must pass to the end. Whether the health of Albrecht Dürer had been injured by home cares and the tongue of Agnes Frey, we know not, though many passages in his letters and journal seem to point to this fact. He died on the 6th of April, 1528, and was buried in the cemetery of St. John at Nuremberg. The scene of his last resting-place is described as being excessively gloomy, unbrightened by grass or flowers. "The tombs, ranged in long rows, like the beds of patients in a hospital, are merely flat stones laid over the graves." In this unlovely spot Albrecht Dürer was laid to sleep beneath the simple epitaph :

'Me. AL. Du.
Quidquid Alberti Dureri mortale fuit
Sub hoc conditur tumulo.
Emigravit VIII. Idus Aprilis, MDXXVIII."

His faithful friend and comforter, Pirkheimer, pronounced his funeral oration, and said of him, that "he united every virtue in his soul—genius, uprightness, purity, energy and prudence, gentleness and piety." The friend who spoke so lovingly was afterwards buried by Dürer's side.

Albrecht Dürer, the versatile genius, who was, like Leonardo
da Vinci, sculptor, engraver, and architect, as well as a painter,
was emphatically *the* Master of his age.   It was, as we have seen,
the age of new life.   The age of Columbus and Sebastian Cabot,
the discoverers.   The age when Luther and Melancthon were
hurling defiance at the old world religion.   The age when Lauren-
tius in Haarlem, and Caxton in Westminster, were setting up
their presses to teach the world.   The age when the learning
which the Moors had cultivated amid the beauties of Granada
was becoming known.   It was the age of Raphael in Italy, of
Sir Thomas More in England ; the age of Germany's brightest
glory.   It was an age instinct with life, thought, and beauty,
and it found its fit representative in the great master, with the
handsome features, and the magic hand, of which it may be said
truly, as it was of another, he touched nothing which he did not
adorn.

Albrecht Dürer represents all the various lights and shades of
German character.   The thought, the inquiring mind, the solid
sense, the weird superstition of the old northern forests, all find
expression in the master's work.   Although it is not certain that
he ever left the Communion of Rome, yet he stands as the artist
of the dawning Reformation.   Melancthon was his friend, and
said of him after his death, " I grieve for Germany, deprived of
such a man, and such an artist.   His least merit was his art."

Most of Dürer's works are to be found in Germany.   In the
Louvre there are only three or four drawings.   The Museum of
Madrid possesses several of his paintings—a *Crucifixion* (1513),
showing the maturity of his genius, two *Allegories* of the same
type as the *Dance of Death*, so favourite a subject at this period,
and a *Portrait of Himself*, bearing the date 1496.   At Munich
we may trace, in a series of seventeen pictures, the dawn, the
noonday, and the evening of Albrecht Dürer's art.   The *Portrait
of his Father*, 1497, is one of his earliest works.   His father was
then seventy years old.   The colour is warm and harmonious.

FIG. 8.—St. John and St. Peter.   St. Paul and St. Mark.
By Albrecht Dürer.   In the Pinakothek at Munich.

A *Portrait of Himself* (1500), placed him, before he was thirty, in the first rank of artists. A *Portrait of Michael Wolgemut,* his old master, comes next in order. Turning from portraits to historical pictures, we find at Munich a *Descent from the Cross,* in which special prominence is given to Joseph of Arimathea, and where the aspect of the dead Christ is terrible from its reality; and a *Nativity,* forming the centre of a triptych, of which the wings have been taken off. The masterpiece of Dürer's art, however, is the painting of the four apostles—*St. John, St. Peter, St. Paul, and St. Mark* (Fig. 8). This wonderful work is clearly the production of his later years; it bears no date, but the absence of the hardness, which Michael Wolgemut's work-shop had imparted to his early style, is gone, and the whole work shows the influence of his travels and unflagging study. It is usually assigned to the year 1526. The picture has been supposed to represent the *Four Temperaments,* but there is no satisfactory proof that Dürer intended this.

Vienna possesses some of the finest specimens of his art. In the legend of *The Ten Thousand Martyrs,* who were slain by the Persian king Shahpour II., Dürer has described on a panel of about a foot square every conceivable kind of torture; these horrors are witnessed by two figures which represent the painter himself, and his friend Pirkheimer. The difficulty of treating such a subject is immense; the execution, finish, and colouring of the picture are marvellous. The date is 1508.

The *Adoration of the Trinity* is one of the most famous of Dürer's works (Fig. 9). It is a vast allegorical picture representing the Christian Religion. The other part of the work depicts the Three Persons of the Blessed Trinity attended by angels; a little lower appear the holy women of all time on one side; the saints, patriarchs, prophets, apostles, and martyrs on the other. Lower still appear the pope, bishops, priests, monks, and nuns —in a word, the Church. Opposite appear the Emperor, and the various ranks which represent the State. Below is a peaceful

FIG. 9.—THE TRINITY. BY DÜRER.
In the Belvedere, Vienna.

view of earth and sea, and the Master himself is represented
gazing on the scene, with his hand resting on a tablet which
bears the date 1511. In this vast work appear the many-sided
forms of Dürer's genius. The real and the ideal, the sublime
and the grotesque, are all represented.

No painter has had more pictures attributed to him falsely
than Albrecht Dürer; but his fame rests not so much upon the
paintings which he really executed as upon his engravings; to
those who are acquainted with him only through the latter his
pictures are frequently at first sight disappointing. Of his
wood-cuts the best known are the *Apocalypse*, 1498; the *Life
of the Virgin*, 1511; and the *History of Christ's Passion*.
Of his copper-plate engravings, *St. Hubert; St. Jerome;* and
The Knight, Death, and the Devil, bearing the date 1513, in
which we see what Kugler calls "the most important work
which the fantastic spirit of German Art has ever produced."
The weird, the terrible, and the grotesque look forth from this
picture like the forms of some horrible nightmare. Another
famous engraving, called *Melancholy*, is full of mystic poetry: it
bears the date 1514. To these may be added a series of 16 drawings in pen and ink on grey paper, heightened with white, representing *Christ's Passion*, which he never engraved. They are in
his best style, and among the finest of his works.

Among the principal pupils and followers of Albrecht Dürer,
was HANS BURCKMAIR,* born at Augsburg, in 1473, who was in
early life a pupil of Schongauer. He painted in two styles;
the one purely German in character, and somewhat hard in
execution, is represented favourably in a picture of *Christ on
the Mount of Olives*. A picture of himself and his wife in the
Belvedere Gallery, at Vienna, is of the same character (Fig. 10).
His second style is more harmonious, and more Italian, and is
shown in the *Adoration of the Kings*, in the Augsburg Gallery.
Burckmair, who died at Augsburg in 1531, was also celebrated

* Or Burgkmair.

FIG. 10.—HANS BURCKMAIR AND HIS WIFE. BY BURCKMAIR.
In the Belvedere, Vienna.

as an engraver; he is, indeed, best known by the splendid series
of wood-cuts of the *Triumph of the Emperor Maximilian;* a
continuous procession in more than 100 plates, remarkable, even

FIG. 11.—A KNIGHT. BY BURCKMAIR.

among the numerous fine works of that period, for prolific invention, and boldness and freedom of execution.

HANS FUSS,* called from his birth-place HANS VON KULMBACH,
is styled by Kugler "one of the most pleasing of Albrecht
Dürer's scholars." He was working in that painter's studio as

* Not Wagner, the name usually given to him.

late as 1518. He died at Nuremberg about 1522. His master-piece is a *Madonna and Child adored by Saints*, in the church of St. Sebald, at Nuremberg.

HANS LEONHARDT SCHÄUFELIN (1490—1540) was Albrecht Dürer's favourite pupil, and many of his works have been attri-buted to his master. A *St. Bridget* in the chapel of St. Maurice, at Nuremberg, is one of the most remarkable of his very unequal works.

Seven artists, who were both painters and engravers, but especially engravers, and who followed in the steps of Albrecht Dürer, are known from the smallness of their works as

THE LITTLE MASTERS.

ALBRECHT ALTDORFER, who was born before 1480, was the creator of landscape painting in Germany. Leaving Bavaria, his birth-place, he settled in Ratisbon, and received the citizenship in 1505. He was an architect of great skill, as well as an engraver on wood and copper. His masterpiece is the *Victory of Alexander over Darius*, painted in 1529 for Duke Wilhelm IV. of Bavaria, and is said to contain more figures than any other picture. Schlegel calls it "a little world on a few feet of canvas." It is in the Munich Gallery. Altdorfer died at Ratisbon in 1538.

BARTHEL BEHAM, who was born at Nuremberg in 1502, also painted under the patronage of Duke Wilhelm IV. He was a close follower of Albrecht Dürer in his earlier works, but his style is coarsely realistic. He was sent to Italy by his patron, and died in that country suddenly about 1540. His earlier style, copied from Dürer, is represented in a *Christ on the Mount of Olives*, in the Berlin Gallery. *A Woman raised from the Dead by the True Cross*, in the Munich Gallery, displays his later or Italianized style.

HANS SEBALD BEHAM, who was born at Nuremberg in 1500, was the elder brother of Barthel. He left Nuremberg under a cloud of disgrace in 1530, and settled in Frankfort. Only one of his oil paintings is known; it represents, on the top of a table, four *Scenes in the Life of David*, and was painted for Albrecht, Archbishop of Mayence; it is now in the Louvre. Hans Beham possessed great powers of invention, and sometimes used them without much care for delicacy or decency. We give as an illustration a copy of one of his engravings (Fig. 12), which are very numerous, and are marvels of minuteness and brilliant effect.

FIG. 12.—LUXURIOUS LIVING. BY HANS SEBALD BEHAM.

GEORG PENCZ, who was born about 1500, was famous as an engraver as well as a painter; his pictures are very rare. In Italy he studied the works of Raphael, and learned engraving under Marcantonio, and is supposed to have executed many works that pass under the name of this master; among others the famous *Massacre of the Innocents*. His portraits are remarkable. His German style is shown in a *St. Jerome*, in the Chapel of St. Maurice, at Nuremberg. The Gallery of Munich has an excellent specimen of his Italian style in a *Venus and Cupid*. Among his engravings are an admirable series illustrating the *History of Tobit*. Pencz died in his native Nuremberg, in 1550.

Fig. 13.—John of Leyden.
From the Engraving by Aldegrever.

HEINRICH ALDEGREVER was born in 1502, in Westphalia, probably at Paderborn, and is said to have left his home to study under Albrecht Dürer,* whose works he had seen. He imitated this master so successfully that he acquired the name of "Albrecht von Westphalen." He died in 1558, it is supposed, at Soest, where he had spent the greater part of his life. Of his works, the *Portrait of a young Man*, dated 1544, in the Liechtenstein Gallery at Vienna, and a *Resurrection*, in the Museum of Prague, are most noteworthy. He engraved portraits of *Luther, Melancthon*, and *John of Leyden* (Fig. 13).

JAKOB BINK, who was born at Cologne between 1490 and 1504, was more famous as an engraver than a painter. He was appointed painter to Christian III., king of Denmark, and produced portraits of the king, and of his queen, Dorothea, which are said to be at Copenhagen. Prince Albrecht of Brandenburg employed Bink to erect a monument, and he was still in that prince's service when he died at Königsberg in 1568, or 1569. No other pictures of this artist, except portraits, are known.

HANS BROSAMER (born at Fulda in 1506) was an excellent engraver on wood and copper.

Among the little masters who were engravers only we may mention the names of VIRGILIUS SOLIS (1154—1562), JOST AMMAN (1539—1591), and THEODOR DE BRY (1528—1598); they were chiefly celebrated for their decorative art.

THE SCHOOL OF SAXONY.

IT will be convenient here to speak of a master who was contemporary with Albrecht Dürer—LUCAS CRANACH, who was born in 1472, was so named from his birthplace, Kronach, in Franconia : with him and his son, Lucas " the younger," begins and ends the School of Saxony. Cranach has been called Lucas Sunder; but this name, it is now said, is a mistaken one.

* Rosenberg thinks that he was never a pupil of Dürer, and, moreover, never even visited Nuremberg.

FIG. 14.—CHRIST AND THE WOMAN TAKEN IN ADULTERY. BY CRANACH.

In the Pinakothek, Munich.

Lucas Cranach had a prosperous and honoured life. At twenty-one years old he accompanied Frederick the Wise, Elector of Saxony, to the Holy Land. In 1495, on their return, the painter had apartments in the Elector's palace at Wittenberg, and was subsequently elected Burgomaster. He held that office again from 1540 to 1544, and was successively Court-painter to three Electors—Frederick the Wise, John the Constant, and John Frederick the Magnanimous. When the last-named prince was taken prisoner by Charles V. at the battle of Mühlberg, the painter, it is said, chose to share his patron's five years' captivity rather than enjoy the favours of the conqueror.* He died at Weimar in 1553. He was early a convert to Protestantism, and was a friend of Luther. His works have none of the dark, weird mystery which belongs to his great rival Albrecht Dürer. All Cranach's paintings are, with a few exceptions, to be found in Germany. At Munich is a large picture, the *Woman taken in Adultery* (Fig. 14), the face of the principal personage being thoroughly German in type, whilst some of the faces of the spectators display that grotesqueness which is one mark of Lucas Cranach's style. Among his smaller works, which are indeed his best, are *Adam and Eve in Paradise*, and *Lot and his Daughters in a grotto*, both at Munich. He was fond of painting nude figures, and often with a ludicrous result; for, from his primitive style of drawing, combined with his German *naïveté* and want of perception of the beautiful, his Eves and Venuses sometimes present a most comic appearance; especially when, as is occasionally to be seen, he crowns these otherwise unadorned beauties with a large crimson velvet hat. Berlin possesses the best collection of works by this master; *Hercules and Omphale*, and the *Fountain of Youth*, are typical specimens of his style, which is thoroughly realistic. A *Portrait of a Young Girl*, in the National Gallery, displays the sweet, simple female face which Cranach delighted to paint. He excelled also in hunting scenes : he is even better known as an

* Modern writers doubt the truth of this statement.

engraver than a painter. His tombstone bears the epitaph,
"Celerrimus Pictor," in compliment to his rapid hand.

LUCAS CRANACH "the Younger" (born at Wittenberg in
1515), the son of the last-named master, was a student of his
father, and of Albrecht Dürer. He preserved his originality,
and avoided the seductions of the Italian School so fatal to
many of his countrymen. Many works attributed to the elder
Cranach were doubtless painted by the son; notably a *Virgin
and Child* in the Munich Gallery. A *Crucifixion of Christ with
the Thieves*, and a *Nativity.* in the Church of Wittenberg, are
certainly from his hand. He died in that city in 1586.

FIG. 15.—MADONNA OF THE CRESCENT MOON. BY ALDEGREVER.

THE PEASANTS' DANCE. BY HOLBEIN.

CHAPTER IV.

HANS HOLBEIN AND HIS SUCCESSORS.

(1497—1560.)

NEXT to the town of Nuremberg, the home of Albrecht Dürer, Augsburg claims our notice as the birth-place of Hans Holbein, a master of the German School, second only to him of Nuremberg, and one perhaps even more typical of the Protestant artists of the Reformation. Though a German in thought and work, he belongs chiefly to England, where he laboured, and where he died obscurely. He was far more Protestant in his art than Albrecht Dürer; the traditions of the Middle Ages which clung around Dürer are totally wanting in Holbein, who painted the portraits of his patrons under the guise of the holiest persons of Gospel history. There has been much confusion about the dates of the life and work of this master, which, thanks to the exertions of Dr. Alfred Woltmann, has of late years been made clear.

Holbein was born and nurtured in an atmosphere of art. His father, HANS HOLBEIN "the elder," laboured under the disadvantage of having a famous son. Himself a painter, many of his works have been attributed to his child; and it is only under the

FIG. 16.—SAINT BARBARA.   SAINT ELIZABETH.
From the St. Sebastian altar-piece by Hans Holbein the elder at Munich.

microscope of recent criticism and careful investigation, that the elder Holbein has found justice. The altar-piece of *St. Sebastian* in the Munich Gallery, for example, was always believed to be the work of the son, till an inscription upon it was proved to be a forgery. On one of the wings of this altar-piece is an *Annunciation*, on the other *St. Barbara* and *St. Elizabeth* (Fig. 16). His brother, Sigmund Holbein, was also a member of the craft.

HANS HOLBEIN "the younger" was born in Augsburg, in 1497. Comparing him with Albrecht Dürer, Kugler says that "as respects grandeur and depth of feeling, and richness of his invention and conception in the field of ecclesiastical art, he stands below the great Nuremberg painter. Though not unaffected by the fantastic element which prevailed in the Middle Ages, Holbein shows it in his own way." What we know of Holbein's life must be told briefly. He was painting independently, and for profit, when only fifteen. He was only twenty when he left Augsburg, and went to Bâle. There he painted his earliest known works, which still remain there. They are *The Last Supper;* a *Flagellation;* the *Portraits of Jacob Meyer and his Wife;* and others, less important. In 1519, after a visit to Lucerne, we find him a member of the Guild of Painters at Bâle, and years later he was painting frescoes for the walls of the Rathaus—frescoes which have yielded to damp and decay, and of which fragments only remain. These are in the Museum of Bâle, as well as eight scenes from *The Passion,* which belong to the same date. In 1522, Holbein painted the *Virgin and Child between St. Martin and St. Ursus*—a picture discovered by Mr. Zetter, of Solothurn, in 1865. It was once an altar-piece in the Church of Grenchen in the Canton of Solothurn, and is one of the most favourable specimens of Holbein's art. Doubtless, Holbein had gone to Bâle poor, and in search of any remunerative work. It is said that he and his brother Ambrose visited that city with the hope of finding employment in illustrating books, an art for which Bâle was famous. Hans Holbein was destined, however,

FIG. 17.—THE MADONNA OF THE MEYER FAMILY. BY HOLBEIN.
In the Dresden Gallery.

to find a new home and new patrons. The last work of importance executed at this time was the *Meyer Madonna*, one of the
most famous of his works. This picture is in the possession of
Prince Hesse of Darmstadt, and the *Meyer Madonna* at Dresden
(Fig. 17) is now acknowledged by the best authorities to be a
replica of the Darmstadt picture. The latter was painted for
the Burgomaster, Jacob Meyer of Bâle. The Protestant Virgin
and the form of the Holy Child amid the Burgomaster's family,
are typical proofs that Holbein was the painter of the new faith
of the Reformation.

Shortly we find him in the land where that faith was being
enforced with no gentle hand, and where the best and noblest
men kept their heads on their shoulders with difficulty. In 1526,
Holbein went to England. The house of Sir Thomas More
in Chelsea received him, and there he worked as an honoured
guest—painting portraits of the ill-fated Chancellor and his
family. Of other portraits painted at this time that of *Sir Bryan
Tuke*, treasurer of the king's chamber, now in the collection of
the Duke of Westminster, and that of *Archbishop Warham*,
in the Louvre, are famous specimens. There is a replica
of Archbishop Warham's portrait in Lambeth Palace. Having
returned to Bâle for a season, hard times forced Holbein to seek
work once more in England. This was in 1532, when he was
taken into the service of Henry VIII., a position not without
its dangers. He was appointed court-painter at a salary of £34
a-year, with rooms in the palace. The amount of this not very
magnificent stipend is proved from an entry in a book at the
Chamberlain's Office, which under the date 1538 contains these
words:—"Payd to Hans Holbein, Paynter, a quarter due at
Lady Day last, £8 10s. 9d."

Holbein was employed to celebrate the marriage of Anne
Boleyn by painting two pictures in tempera in the Banqueting
Hall of the Easterlings at the Steelyard. He chose the favourite
subjects for such works, *The Triumph of Riches*, and *The Triumph*

FIG. 18.—PORTRAIT OF CHRISTINA, DUCHESS OF MILAN. BY HOLBEIN.
At Arundel Castle.

[The Original is a full-length portrait.]

of Poverty. The pictures probably perished in the Great Fire of London. In 1538, Holbein was engaged on a very delicate mission, considering the matrimonial peculiarities of his royal master. He was sent to Brussels to paint the *Portrait of Christina,* widow of Francesco Sforza, Duke of Milan, whom Henry would have made his queen, had she been willing. This portrait (Fig. 18), now in the possession of the Duke of Norfolk,* was the theme of much praise at the Winter Exhibition of the Old Masters at Burlington House, 1879-80. Soon after, having refused an earnest invitation from Bâle to return there, Holbein painted an aspirant to the royal hand, Anne of Cleves. Perhaps the painter flattered the lady; at all events the original was so distasteful to the king that he burst into a fit of rage which cost Thomas Cromwell his head. Holbein continued his work as a portrait painter, and has left us many memorials of the Tudor Court. He died in 1543 of the plague, but nothing is known of his burial-place. Some time before his death we hear of him as a resident in the parish of St. Andrew Undershaft, in the city.

The fame of this great master rests almost entirely upon his power as a portrait painter. In the collection of drawings at Windsor, mostly executed in red chalk and Indian ink, we are introduced to the chief personages who lived in and around the splendid court in the troublous times of the second Tudor. There are several good specimens of Holbein's art among the drawings in the British Museum, but he was unrepresented in the National Gallery until 1880, when the Trustees acquired a portrait of *Martin Luther†* which is attributed to him. Famous among his works are his designs for the *Dance of Death,* which were engraved on wood by Hans Lützelburger; some authorities however maintain that Holbein actually cut the designs with his own hand. The weird and grotesque side of German art is

* Replicas at Windsor Castle and at Castle Howard are also claimed to be the original painting. The Duke of Norfolk's picture is at present (1881) on loan in the National Gallery.

† Not yet exhibited (*April,* 1881).

shown at its best in these pictures, where Death summons all classes alike — kings and peasants, priests and paladins, fair women and tender children—to join his ghastly revelry.

Holbein has had a vast number of pictures falsely assigned to him. It was formerly believed that he died in 1554 instead of in 1543, and numerous works executed between these dates are now proved to have been from another hand.

Probably from the fact that he early left his native land to live in England, Holbein founded no school of painting Among his imitators we may mention CHRISTOPHER AMBERGER, who was born about 1490, and was a native of Augsburg : he studied under the elder Holbein, but learnt more from the works of the younger. He painted the portrait of the Emperor Charles V., in 1532, and that monarch declared the work was as good as that of Titian. The original is in the Institute of Fine Arts at Siena, and is there ascribed to Holbein. The one at Berlin is a replica by Amberger. This artist also painted historical works, but his power lay chiefly in portraiture. He died at Augsburg in 1563.

NICOLAUS MANUEL, known also as DEUTSCH, was born about 1484, at Berne, and was famous not only as a painter but as a reformer, a soldier, a poet, and a statesman. He studied under Titian in Italy, and shows the influence of the great master in the richness of colour in his backgrounds. Manuel painted forty-six large frescoes on the walls of a Dominican convent at Berne, choosing the ever popular *Dance of Death* as his subject. But Death here appears in a pleasant, even humorous form, adapting himself to the tastes of his victims, and making the inevitable journey as agreeable as may be. These frescoes have perished, but copies have been published at Berne The museum at Bâle contains many fine specimens of this painter's art. He died at Berne in 1530.

THE FOX-CHASE. BY HOLBEIN.

CHAPTER V.

THE DECADENCE AND REVIVAL OF GERMAN ART.
(1550—1880.)

THE glory of German art died out with Albrecht Dürer. The very versatility of that master's genius prevented him from forming a school. His imitators copied, with more or less success, his various styles, and thus diverged widely in different directions. After the death of Dürer, of Holbein, and of Cranach, the national art which had flourished at Nuremberg, at Augsburg, at Ulm, and Cologne, fell into a sleep from which the awakening was long delayed. The various painters of Germany became mere copyists of the Italian Schools. Thus of HEINRICH GOLTZIUS (1558—1617), it has been said, that "he struggled after Michelangelo in distorted dreams."

JOHANN ROTTENHAMMER * (1564—1623) was a copyist of Tintoretto. He was patronised by the Emperor Rudolph II., but died at Augsburg in poverty. A *Death of Adonis* (in the Louvre), and a *Pan and Syrinx* (National Gallery), with the background painted by Jan Brueghel, are favourable specimens of his art.

* Sometimes written Rotlenhammer.

ADAM ELSHAIMER * (1574—1620) excelled as a landscape painter. It is said that his memory was so powerful, that, after once seeing a landscape, he could reproduce it on canvas perfect in every detail. His works were appreciated after his death, but in life he had only two patrons, of whom Rubens was one ; he died a pauper, in Rome. The masterpiece of Elshaimer is a *Flight into Egypt* in the Louvre ; many of his best pictures are in private collections in England.

FIG. 19.—ALEXANDER'S HORSE. BY SANDRART.
From a design in his " Academia nobilissimæ Artis pictoriæ."

JOACHIM VON SANDRART was born at Frankfort in 1606, and commenced life as an engraver. Having abandoned the graver for the brush, he studied first at Utrecht, and then at Venice and Rome. On his return to Germany after many years' absence he executed several altar-pieces for churches in Bavaria and Austria. In the Belvedere at Vienna there is a famous picture by Sandrart,

* Often written Elzheimer.

D 2

entitled the *Allegory* : it represents Pallas and Saturn defending the Genii of Fine Arts against the Furies of Envy. Another of his great pictures is in the town-hall of Amsterdam, and shows us a company of the *Amsterdam Archers at the Entry of Marie de Medicis*. Sandrart, however, is more famous for his history of Teutonic art, the *Teutsche Academie* (published at Nuremberg, 1675), than for his pictures. He died at Nuremberg in 1688.

BALTHASAR DENNER was born at Altona in 1685. Little is known of his life. He studied under obscure masters at Altona and Dantzic ; and wandered from one German court to another with varying success. He visited England, but was not appreciated. Denner was a painter of microscopic exactness. He could spend days of loving labour over a wrinkle, and hang fondly over the delineation of a hair. His portraits are those of heads simply, cut off below the chin, and to these he gave by his minute labour an accuracy which is perfectly frightful. "A thing of beauty" was by no means "a joy for ever" to Denner. He preferred the wrinkled skin of some toothless patriarch to the velvet cheek of the loveliest maiden. As a portrait painter he was much prized, and among his works are the portraits of *Peter III. of Russia, Augustus II. of Poland*, and *Frederick IV. of Denmark*. In the Vienna Gallery are a *Portrait of Himself*, and a *Head of an Old Woman*, for which latter work the Emperor Charles VI. gave Denner four thousand seven hundred florins. He died at Rostock in 1747.

CHRISTIAN WILHELM ERNST DIETRICH,* who was born at Weimar in 1712, became court painter to Augustus II. of Poland, and to his successor Augustus III. He studied in Rome, and on his return was made keeper of the Dresden Gallery, and Professor in the Academy of Arts in the same city. He was a popular and successful man throughout his life, and yet he never painted an original picture. He was a universal copyist. The

* Or Dietricij, as he is said to have written it himself about 1733 after his visit to Italy.

FIG. 20.—THE KNIFE-GRINDER.

From an Engraving by Dietrich.

verdict of Michelangelo on Baccio Bandinelli applies equally
to Dietrich : " Who walks behind another, will never pass him
by." He walked behind numberless masters. In the illustration we have given from an engraving by himself, *The Knife-
Grinder* (Fig. 20), the influence of Van Ostade is plainly dis-
cernible. If we look at his fifty-one works in the Dresden

FIG. 21.—THE RAT-CATCHER. BY DIETRICH.

Gallery, we shall see Gerard Dou in *The Young Woman and
her Children*, and recognize Van der Werff in the *Golden Age*.
The shadow of Salvator Rosa falls upon the *Cuirassiers on a
March*, and a memory of Raphael haunts an Italian landscape
with a *Holy Family*. Adriaan van Ostade, Jan Both, Watteau,
Dujardin, and many another look at us from the canvases of

FIG. 22.—ST. PETER. BY MENGS.
In the Gallery of the Belvedere, Vienna.

Dietrich. His best picture in England is *The Itinerant Musicians,* in the National Gallery. He died at Dresden in 1774.

ANTON RAPHAEL MENGS (1728—1779) was born at Aussig, in Bohemia. If it could not be said of him that "he lisped in numbers," it was true that his earliest plaything was a pencil. His father, who was a miniature painter, had determined that his son should be an artist, and named him after Correggio and Sanzio. As a little child Raphael Mengs was sent to study the masters in the gallery of Dresden, whither his father had removed. Thence, when only thirteen, the boy was taken to Rome, and was shut up in the Vatican all day long with a crust of bread and a can of water. Thus the path of art was not strewn with roses for Raphael Mengs. When quite a youth he became court painter to Augustus III., King of Poland and Elector of Saxony, who allowed him to continue his studies in Rome. There he painted a *Holy Family,* taking as his model for the Virgin a peasant girl whom he married, changing his creed to accommodate the feelings of his wife. In 1761 Mengs visited Madrid at the invitation of Charles III., and executed many of his greatest works among them the *Apotheosis of Trajan,* on the ceiling of the dining-hall of the palace at Madrid. Once more in Rome for a space of three years, we find Mengs painting his famous *Allegory* on the ceiling of the Camera de' Papini. He was in Spain till 1775, when he again visited Rome, and then having lost his wife in 1778, Mengs died within a year, of grief and unskilful medical treatment. With all the advantages of his early training and laborious youth, with all the care and study of the antique which he lavished upon his work, Mengs lacked the two qualities which make a great painter—originality and warmth. Although he shows signs of the art of better days, in a period of degradation, he is always cold and lifeless even in his greatest works. It is strange that Winckelmann, the distinguished critic of ancient art, should have had no more insight into this fact than to affirm that Mengs was the greatest painter of that " or

FIG. 23.—BLIND MAN'S BUFF. BY ANGELICA KAUFFMAN.

perhaps of any age." His pictures are rare in France, there are some in Saxony and Italy, and the greatest number in Spain. His masterpiece is an *Adoration of the Shepherds* in the Museo del Rey at Madrid. Two *Portraits of Himself* in the Munich Gallery, another in the Uffizi, and a *Portrait of his Father* at Berlin, and his picture of *St. Peter* in the Belvedere Gallery at Vienna (Fig. 22), show his power in this department of art. He was also the author of 'Thoughts on Painting, and Reflections on Painters.'

ANGELICA KAUFFMAN was born at Schwartzenberg, in the Bregenzer Wald, Austria,* in 1741. At the age of 15 she was taken by her father to Milan, to improve in the arts of music and painting, and in 1763-4 she visited Naples and Rome, and became known as a portrait painter. The Abbé Winckelmann, who sat to her, mentions Angelica Kauffman with the highest praise. After visiting Venice she came to England in 1765 with Lady Wentworth, wife of the British Ambassador. Here she was soon the centre of a brilliant society, and was equally famous for her wit, her amiability, and her power as a portrait painter. She also painted fanciful subjects, of which *Blind Man's Buff* is a characteristic example (Fig. 23). In 1768 she achieved the honour of being elected one of the original members of the Royal Academy. Her unfortunate marriage with an impostor, calling himself Count Horn, and her subsequent union to her first love, Antonio Zucchi, which also proved unfortunate, have cast a glamour of romance over this artist's life. She returned to Rome, and devoted herself very successfully to historical painting till her death in 1807. The works of Angelica Kauffman are rather pleasing than powerful. Fifteen of her pictures are in the collection of Lord Exeter.

ASMUS JAKOB CARSTENS (1754—1798) was one of the best German painters of the period immediately preceding the revival

---

* Chur (Coire), in the Grisons, has until recently been supposed to be the place of her birth. See *Athenæum*, No. 2733.

FIG. 24.—THE FATES—NEMESIS, NIGHT, AND DESTINY. BY CARSTENS.
In the Weimar Museum.

of German Art. The son of a miller, he was apprenticed to a wine merchant, and throughout his life had a hard struggle with fortune. He travelled to Copenhagen, and there procured a precarious livelihood by drawing portraits in red chalk. Two pictures painted at this time, however, attracted favourable notice, *The Death of Balder*, and *Ulysses and Æolus;* but the good fortune which seemed to await him was darkened by an unfortunate quarrel with the artists of the place. At Berlin, Carstens painted his *Fall of the Angels*, and was made a member of the Academy, and in 1792 received a travelling pension from the Court. After studying the works of Dürer at Dresden and Nuremberg, he visited Rome, and as the result of his studies there painted his *Visit of the Argonauts to the Centaur Chiron*. Carstens chiefly dealt with mythology in his pictures, and was a careful student of Raphael and Michelangelo. His *Fates—Nemesis, Night, and Destiny*, in the Weimar Museum (Fig. 24), is an excellent example of his style.

REVIVAL OF ART IN GERMANY.

"THE Germans—who joined in the European work of a fresh Revival of Art twenty years later than the French under Louis David—undertook their mission in an entirely different spirit. Instead of carrying Art forward, they turned back, and rather than go on resolutely to the discovery of an unknown future, thought it more prudent to return to the past, and to take refuge in archaism. At the death of Albrecht Dürer, artistic Germany fell asleep as if in the cavern of Epimenides. Aroused at last by the rumour of the revival of the arts in France, she resumed her task where it had been left at the close of the fifteenth century. It was to Rome that she once more turned in order to rekindle the extinguished flame. The history of the little German colony is well known which, in 1810, crossed the mountains under the direction of Friedrich Overbeck, and established at Rome a convent of artists, where all the subsequent heads of

FIG. 25.—THE CALLING OF JAMES AND JOHN. BY OVERBECK.

schools were formed, Peter von Cornelius, Wilhelm Schadow, Philipp Veit, Julius Schnorr, Karl Vogel, Heinrich Hess, and others less worthy of mention. They followed to the letter the paradoxical advice of Lanzi, that 'modern artists should study the painters of the time preceding Raphael; for Raphael, spring-ing from these painters, is superior to them, whilst those who followed him have not equalled him.' Their enthusiasm for what they called the 'Christian ideal,' for Art anterior to the religious reformation, led them even to renounce the religion of their fathers. The Protestants became Catholics, and Overbeck, who set the example of abjuration as well as exile, was not satis-fied with returning to the age of Leo X., but endeavoured to adapt, to the mystic style of Fra Angelico, the types of Raphael, in which Grecian beauty is visible.

" This influence imprinted on German painting an irremediable defect; to avoid the fault with which they reproached the Dutch —that of not knowing how to *idealise the real*—the Germans fell into the opposite extreme, of being unable to *realise the ideal*. Happily, they have not persisted in this blind alley, where progress was impossible. The schools of Düsseldorf and Munich have produced noble painters who, by turning to pic-turesque truth, have returned to their own times and their own country."—Viardot.

JOHANN FRIEDRICH OVERBECK, the chief of the Revivalists of German art, was born at Lübeck in 1789. When about eighteen years of age he went to Vienna, to study painting in the Academy of that city. The ideas on art which he had carried with him were so entirely new and so little agreeable to the professors of the Academy, that they met with but small approval. On the other hand, there were several among his fellow-pupils who gladly followed his lead; and in 1810, Overbeck, accompanied by a small band of youthful artists, went to Rome, where he estab-lished the school which was afterwards to become so famous.

Overbeck, who was professor of painting in the Academy of

St. Luke, a foreign member of the French Institute, and a member of all the German Academies, died at Rome in 1869, at the advanced age of eighty years.   He painted both in fresco and in oil.   Of his productions in fresco, the most noteworthy are, a *Vision of St. Francis* in Santa Maria degli Angeli, at Assisi, and five scenes from Tasso's *Jerusalem Delivered*, in the villa of the Marchese Massimo, in Rome.   Of his oil-paintings the best are the *Triumph of Religion in the Arts* in the Städel Institute at Frankfort; *Christ on the Mount of Olives* at Hamburg; the *Entrance of Christ into Jerusalem*, painted in 1816 for the Marien Kirche at Lübeck; and a *Descent from the Cross*, at Lübeck. Overbeck also executed a number of small drawings.   Of these we may mention forty designs of the *Life of Christ* (Fig. 25), and many other Biblical subjects.

PETER VON CORNELIUS, one of the greatest of modern German painters, was born at Düsseldorf in 1783, and first studied art in the gallery of his native city, of which his father was inspector. In 1811 he went to Rome and joined the school which Overbeck had previously established there.   After several years of study in the Papal capital, Cornelius was commissioned by the then Crown Prince of Bavaria to paint various frescoes for the Glyptothek of Munich.   Accompanied by a few pupils, he repaired to Munich where, in 1824 or 1825, he was made Director of the Academy.   He died in 1867 at Rome.   His pictures mostly represent scenes from the Old and New Testament, the *Nibelungenlied*, and the works of great writers—Homer, Dante, Göthe, and others.   We may especially notice some frescoes, representing the *History of Man* from the Creation to the Last Judgment, in the Ludwigs Kirche at Munich.   The *Four Riders of the Apocalypse*, designed for the Campo Santo at Berlin, is one of his best-known compositions (Fig. 26).   Cornelius is not a great colourist, but he excels in grandeur of design.   His figures, though they sometimes have a statue-like appearance, are perfect; and his drawing is worthy of the utmost praise.

FRIEDRICH WILHELM VON SCHADOW, the son of Godefroid Schadow the sculptor, was born at Berlin in 1789. He first studied under a painter named Weitsch, but abandoned that master in favour of Cornelius, whose pupil he must be considered. Schadow was a member of the Academy of Berlin, and also for some time Director of the Düsseldorf Academy. He died at Düsseldorf in 1862. Among his best pictures are, the *Four Evangelists;* a *Deposition;* and also a *Holy Family* at Munich. Schadow was also a portrait painter.

PETER HESS, the " Horace Vernet of Central Germany," was born at Düsseldorf in 1792. He was the son of Karl Hess, the professor of engraving in the Düsseldorf Academy, and the brother of two other artists—Heinrich von Hess, an historical painter, and Karl Hess, a painter of battle-pieces of less note. Peter Hess was, at various times, much patronized by the Bavarian Government. He died at Munich, in 1871. Of his pictures, we may mention the *Entrance of King Otho into Nauplia* in 1833 *;* the *Battle of Arcis-sur-Aube;* and the *Crossing of the Berezina*—painted for the late Emperor of Russia.

PHILIPP VEIT was born at Berlin in 1793. His mother, after the death of her first husband, married the painter Friedrich Schlegel, who thus became Veit's instructor. The young artist studied for some time in Dresden, and then went to Rome, where he became one of the most severe in style of those artists of the revival. Of the works which Veit executed in Rome, the most important is the *Seven years of Plenty*, painted in fresco in the Villa Bartholdy, as companion picture to Overbeck's *Seven years of Dearth.* The works which Veit executed in Rome procured him so much fame in Germany, that he was summoned to Frankfort-on-the-Main to take the Directorship of the Art Institute. Owing to differences in religious opinions, he was · obliged to resign this office in 1843. He then removed to Sachsenhausen in Hesse-Cassel, where he afterwards chiefly resided. He died in 1877, at Mayence. Of

GFDP   E his later works we may mention an *Ascension of the Virgin,* painted for the Frankfort Cathedral, and a *Good Samaritan,* painted for the king of Prussia.

JULIUS SCHNORR VON KAROLSFELD, the third son of Johann Veit Schnorr, the Director of the Academy at Leipsic, was born in 1794, in that city. He was sent in 1810 to the Academy of Vienna, where his two elder brothers were already studying. Schnorr did not, however, find the professors of the Academy at all sympathetic with his desire for the improvement of Art. He accordingly left Vienna and went to Rome in 1815, where his chief works were the *Marriage at Cana* and scenes from *Orlando Furioso* in the Villa Massimo. Just as he had completed this last work he was called by King Ludwig of Bavaria to Munich, where he executed his most celebrated works—Scenes from the *Nibelungenlied* painted in fresco; and the histories of *Charlemagne, Frederic Barbarossa,* and *Rudolf of Hapsburg,* in encaustic. His well-known *Bible Illustrations* (Fig. 27) have made his name very popular in England. Schnorr died in 1872, at Dresden.

HEINRICH MARIA VON HESS was born at Düsseldorf in 1798. He first studied under his father, Karl von Hess, who was professor of engraving in the Düsseldorf Academy. In 1806, young Hess went to Munich, and entered as a student in the Academy of that city. Seven years later appeared his first great works, the *Sepulchre of Christ,* and a *Holy Family,* which attracted the notice of Queen Caroline, who thenceforth became his liberal patroness. In 1821 he received a royal travelling-grant. He went to Italy, where he stayed until 1826, in which year he returned to Munich, and was soon after made Professor of the Academy. In the following year he commenced a series of cartoons for the Allerheiligen Kirche, which he completed in 1837. In 1849, Hess was made Director of the Royal Collection, which post he held until his death, which occurred at Munich, 1863. Among the best known of his works we may mention a *Christ-*

FIG. 27.—CAIN KILLING ABEL. BY SCHNORR VON KAROLSFELD.
(*From the Bible Cuts.*)

mas, painted for Queen Caroline ; and *Faith, Hope,* and *Charity,* painted for the Leuchtenberg Gallery, at St. Petersburg.

WILHELM VON KAULBACH, the great historical painter, was born at Arolsen, a small town in Waldeck, in 1805. He studied Art at Düsseldorf under Cornelius, and acquired from that master a thorough knowledge of design and drawing, more especially of the human figure. He was Cornelius's best and favourite pupil, and when that master removed to Munich, Kaulbach was among those who followed him. Kaulbach painted chiefly large pictures of an historical character. Thanks to photography, these are well-known to the world. Among his most popular works are, *The Battle of the Huns* in the Berlin Museum ; *Apollo and the Muses,* in the Odeon at Munich ; and the wall-painting at Berlin, representing *Homer in Griechenland ;* his drawings for the illustration of Goethe's *Faust* and *Werner,* and the designs for *Reynard the Fox.* His style is bombastic, without feeling for nature, and has the worst faults of the modern German School. Kaulbach died at Munich in 1874.

CARL FRIEDRICH LESSING, who was born in 1808 at Breslau,* was originally intended for an architect, but evincing a strong love of painting, he studied under Rösel and Dähling at Berlin In 1827 he went with Schadow to Düsseldorf. There he speedily became famous both for his masterly landscapes and his historic paintings. The latter show a strong Protestant feeling—three of his masterpieces being scenes inspired by the history of Huss, the reformer. In 1858 Lessing was appointed Director of the Gallery of Art at Carlsruhe, a post which he held until his death in that town in 1880. His works are frequently to be met with in German galleries. At Berlin are *Huss at the Funeral Pyre ; a Hussite Preaching ;* and several good landscapes ; and at Frankfort, in the Städel Gallery, are *Huss before the Council,* and his famous *Oaks of a thousand years.*

* Some writers say at Wartenberg, in Silesia.

PAINTING IN FLANDERS.

FIG. 27A.—PORTRAIT OF JAN VAN EYCK.
One of the 'Justi Judices' in the " Adoration of the Lamb."

BOOK II.

FLEMISH PAINTING.

CHAPTER I.

THE SCHOOLS OF THE NETHERLANDS.   EARLY FLEMISH ART.

THE records of early Flemish art are few and untrustworthy.
Many works perished in the troublous times when Liège
and other cities were sacked by plunderers.   Still we know
that penmanship and miniature painting were practised in the
convents of the Netherlands at a very early period.   A Benedictine chronicle of the ninth century describes the transcripts from
the Gospels or Psalms made by the Abbesses Harlinde and Ren-
hilde.   Wolfram von Eschenbach mentions painters of Maestricht
and Cologne, and there are traces of art in Liège in the tenth and
eleventh centuries.   Lately, wall-paintings have been discovered
at Maestricht, Liège, Huy, Namur, Ghent, Gorcum, and Haarlem,
which are ascribed to the thirteenth and fourteenth centuries.

The thirteenth century produced in Flanders many degraded
specimens of art, chiefly coarse and revolting martyrdoms.   We
know also of certain artists who were described as "painters and
varlets" to the Counts of Flanders and Dukes of Burgundy.
These craftsmen seem to have been employed by these princely

patrons in many different ways, which ranged from the painting of a weathercock or a pennon, to the construction of mechanical toys and traps, the conduct of a secret commission, or the production of a veritable picture. Among these obscure crafts-men we find JEAN VAN DER ASSELT, painter to Louis de Male, at Ghent, from 1364 to 1380, and afterwards employed by Philip the Hardy; to Van der Asselt probably belong the wall-paintings in the chapel of Louis de Male, at Nôtre Dame of Courtrai. JEAN DE BEAUMEZ was "painter and varlet" to Philip the Hardy from 1377 to 1395. JEAN MALWEL occupied the same position in the courts of Philip, and Jean the Fearless from 1397 to 1415. MELCHIOR BROEDERLAM of Ypres was also in the service of the same Philip, from 1382 to 1400. He displays some glimmering of the brighter day which was to dawn for Flemish art under the auspices of the brothers Van Eyck. The wings for an altar-chest, the principal parts of which are preserved in the Museum of Dijon, contain paintings by Broederlam of the *Annunciation*, the *Visitation*, the *Presentation*, and the *Flight into Egypt*, which are remarkable for simplicity, purity, and beauty of colour.

SCHOOL OF BRUGES (1366—1550).

The glory of early Flemish art culminated in the School of Bruges, and in the works of the brothers Huibrecht and Jan van Eyck. Bruges was at this period the most wealthy and splendid city in Flanders. Possessing in Sluys an excellent port, the trade of England, Spain, Italy, Asia, and Africa, and later that of America, poured its wares into Bruges, in exchange for woollen stuffs, and the heavy grain and fat cattle, of which the Flemish town was the mart. Its citizens were wealthy, it was the favourite residence of the free-handed despotic prince and art-patron, Duke Philippe le Bon, and it was thus in every way suited as a home for the Fine Arts.

We know little of the life of HUIBRECHT VAN EYCK. He was born at Maaseyck, in the valley of the Maes, about 1366. Maaseyck, the birthplace of the two brothers Van Eyck, lies to the north of Maestricht, touching on one side the barren Kempenland, and bounded on the other by the pleasant orchards and gardens of the country of Liège. Huibrecht lived partly at Bruges and partly at Ghent, and was a member of the guild of painters in the latter city in 1421. At Ghent he died in 1426, and was buried with great pomp by Judocus Vydt, his patron, in a vault of the chapel of St. Bavon. One of the painter's arms was preserved at St. Bavon as a valuable relic till the middle of the sixteenth century, when it disappeared.* It has been stated that Jan van Eyck invented the art of painting in oils. This, however, is a mistake, as linseed oil was used in painting as early as the eleventh century. Doubtless, however, one great reason for the marvellous success of the brothers Van Eyck is to be attributed to the discovery of a new process of mixing colours with oil, a discovery which probably originated not with Jan van Eyck, but with his elder brother. This new discovery, which was eagerly sought for by the Italian painters, has given us the distinctive colouring known as "the purple of Van Eyck," which ranks with the "gold of Titian," and "the silver of Veronese."

JAN VAN EYCK, or EIJCK—who was born at Maaseyck about

---

* The following is a translation of the quaint epitaph of Huibrecht van Eyck :—" Take warning from me, ye who walk over me : I was as you are, but am now buried dead beneath you. Thus it appears that neither art nor medicine availed me. Art, honour, wisdom, power, riches, are not spared when death comes. Huibrecht van Eyck I was once named, now I am food for worms. Formerly highly-honoured in painting, this all was shortly afterwards turned to nought.

"It was in the year of the Lord one thousand four hundred and twenty-six, on the eighteenth day of September, that I rendered up my soul to God, in suffering. Pray to God for me, ye who love art, that I may attain to His sight. Flee sin, turn to the best, for you must follow me at last."

1390—entered the service of Jean sans Pitié, the famous John of Bavaria, Bishop of Liège. Dying, the bishop sent the painter with a recommendation to Philippe le Bon, Duke of Burgundy, and we find Jan van Eyck installed as "varlet and painter," and acting as confidential friend and companion to that imperious but liberal prince. Whether Jan van Eyck was among the few hundred courtiers who shaved their heads at the duke's command, so that he might not be singular we know not. We do know, however, that the painter received an annual salary of one hundred livres parisis, and that he had two horses for his use, and "a varlet in livery" to attend him. Besides this regular salary, the painter received other monies for secret service performed during various mysterious missions, about which the chroniclers are very reticent.

In 1428, Jan van Eyck was sent to Portugal, with an embassy consisting of Hue de Lannoy, and the Sire de Roubaix, to paint the portrait of Isabel of Portugal, whilst his companions were to negotiate a marriage between the Princess and the Duke of Burgundy. The embassy met with foul weather, and had to put into Sandwich, Plymouth, and Falmouth. Arrived in Portugal, Jan van Eyck painted the portrait of the Princess Isabel, and having sent it to his master, started for a tour through Portugal and Spain, and saw for the first time the rich vegetation of a brighter clime than his own. We can trace the influence of the scenery of Spain and Portugal in some of his later pictures. In 1429, Jan van Eyck was again in Bruges, to be present at the rejoicings at the ducal marriage, when Philippe instituted the order of the Golden Fleece, and to receive from his patron one hundred and fifty livres for his portrait of the princess, and for his "secret service." He now settled in Bruges in a house of his own, and married. In 1434, we find Duke Philippe le Bon standing as sponsor to Van Eyck's daughter, and giving his godchild no fewer than six silver cups. The painter retained the friendship of this liberal patron throughout his life ;

FIG. 28.—CHOIR OF ANGELS. BY HUIBRECHT VAN EYCK.
(*Upper wing of the polyptych in St. Bavon, at Ghent.*)
In the Berlin Gallery.

thc duke frequently visited his studio, and emptied his pockets among the apprentices. Jan van Eyck died at Bruges in 1440.

The greatest work of the School of Bruges, which combines all the characteristics of early Flemish art,—devotion, religious symbolism of a realistic type, power of colour, and mastery of execution, is the famous *Agnus Dei*, or *Adoration of the Mystic Lamb*. This work is a polyptych * of twelve panels, which, with their shutters, form twenty-four pictures divided into two rows, having five panels in the one, and seven in the other. On the frames of the shutters is this inscription :—

> " Hvbertvs e eyck maior qvo nemo repertvs
> Incepit pondvs q̄e Iohannes arte secvndvs
> (Frater perfecit) Ivdoci Vyd prece fretû.
> VersV SeXta MaI Vos CoLLoCat aCta tVerI."

The last line is a chronogram, which tells us that the great work was finished May 6th, 1432. It was commenced by Huibrecht van Eyck for Judocus Vydt as an altar-piece for his chapel at St. Bavon at Ghent. He lived to complete the whole of the top portion of the interior of the altar-piece, which contains pictures of *God Almighty :* on His right hand are *The Virgin*, a choir of *Angels* (Fig. 28), and *Adam ;* on His left are *St. John the Baptist*, *St. Cecilia*, and *Eve*. The whole work was not completed by Jan van Eyck till 1432. Doubtless he was frequently interrupted in his labour by the exigencies of his services, secret and otherwise, to Duke Philippe le Bon.

This great altar-piece was placed in the chapel of the Vydt family in St. Bavon, at Ghent, in the year in which it was finished. In the central compartment we see the *Mystic Lamb* standing on the ark of the covenant, blood flowing from its wounded side. The Holy Spirit hovers as a dove overhead. Angels kneel around, bearing the instruments of the Passion. In front is the fountain of living water, which pours forth a stream to purify

* πολὺς πτὺξ, many fold.

FIG. 29.—THE ADORATION OF THE LAMB. BY JAN VAN EYCK.

The centre-piece of the polyptych in St. Bavon, at Ghent.

the world. In the foreground are placed the great army of
the redeemed, and farther back are crowds of saints and
martyrs.   In the distance we see a city, meant doubtless to
represent the heavenly Jerusalem, its towers and domes standing out against a sky of pale grey, which gradually diverges into
a deeper tint (Fig. 29).   On the wings on either side of the
central picture we see crowds of persons all journeying towards
the Lamb, all fired with the same spirit of devotion.   Hermits.
crusaders, righteous judges, among whom on horseback are
Huibrecht, and Jan van Eyck (Fig. 27A).   Amid the Christian
warriors are Charlemagne, St. George, and Godefroy de Bouillon.
There was originally a picture underneath, representing hell; this
has been lost.   On the external panels of the shutters are the *Angel
of the Annunciation* and the *Holy Virgin*, and beneath *St. John
the Baptist* and *St. John the Evangelist*, with the portraits of
Judocus Vydt and his wife *Isabel Burluut* on either side.   " Of
the technical qualities of this work, no praise can be too
great.   The inventors of the new method of oil-painting seem
at once to have carried it to perfection, and no after-work of
their school exhibits a more thorough mastery over the mechanical medium, or a more complete understanding of the harmony
of colour than this.   The landscape, both in the centre and
the wings, is delicately and faithfully painted; every soft blade
of grass, every flower is depicted with loving care, but we
have not the exaggeration of minute accuracy such as we find
in some of the Van Eyck landscapes " (*Mrs. C. Heaton*).   The
great altar-piece has passed through many vicissitudes.   It
narrowly escaped the sacrilegious hands of Protestant Vandals in
1556.   It was nearly destroyed by fire in 1641.   Joseph of
Austria's sense of propriety being shocked at the sight of the
figures of Adam and Eve, the altar-piece was closed to the eyes
of spectators for some time.   In the wars of Napoleon it was
carried off as booty, and was sent to the Louvre.   In 1814,
when peace was declared, it was once more restored to St. Bavon

at Ghent, but the wings, instead of being joined to the centre, were hid away in a cellar. A priest found them there, and sold them; in time they passed from the purchaser M. Nieuwenhuys to Mr. Solly, from whom they passed to the late King of Prussia; they are now in the Gallery of Berlin. The panels of *Adam* and *Eve*, after a still longer sojourn in the cellar, at last saw the light in 1860 in the Gallery at Brussels. There are many engravings of the centre and side wings of the famous altar-piece.

Next in order of importance to the *Agnus Dei* of St. Bavon is another altar-piece in the Santa Trinita Museum, Madrid, called the *Triumph of the Catholic Church.* " For power of conception and distribution, no picture of the Flemish School," say Messrs. Crowe and Cavalcaselle, in their 'Lives of Flemish Painters,' "approaches this, except the *Agnus Dei* of St. Bavon. It is the creation of a single hand, and the figures are all of similar stature, but of proportions less than those in the central panel of the *Agnus Dei.*" The same writers, as well as Passavant, consider the two figures which watch the overthrow of the Jewish Church, and the triumph of the Christian, to represent the brothers Van Eyck. Otto Mündler considered this work to belong to a later master, but Bürger and the latest critics decide in attributing it to Jan van Eyck.

The *Pala Madonna,* so called from the name of the patron for whom it was painted, the Canon van der Pala, is another famous picture of this master. It is at Bruges, and there is a copy of it in the Antwerp Museum. It bears the date 1436, and represents the Virgin seated on a throne, with St. George standing in complete armour on her right, and St. Donatus in the dress of an archbishop on her left hand. The donor of the picture, Canon van der Pala, kneels a little behind St. George. In the Antwerp Museum is the celebrated picture—or rather drawing in monochrome, though the material is oil-paint—of *St. Barbara* (Fig. 30 ; *frontispiece*), with her emblem, a beautiful Gothic tower, in the background.

Of the other works of Jan van Eyck we must mention a
picture in the Louvre, known as the *Virgin and the Donor*. The
Chancellor Rollin is depicted kneeling, missal in hand, before
the Virgin and Child.   An angel is crowning the Virgin, and a
city resembling Lyons, but probably typical of Jerusalem, is seen
in the distance.   "This picture," says Viardot, "is rather pale
in its general tint, without much relief or depth, and does not
show any of the brilliant colour which is known as the *purple
of Van Eyck*.   In any case it is not one of those which deserve
his short and modest motto, ALS IXH XAN * (*as well as I can*),
for he could do better."   There are two heads of *Christ* painted
by Jan van Eyck, one at Bruges bearing the date 1420, and
displaying the earliest specimen perhaps of the new method of
oil painting, and the other at Berlin, dated 1438.   In England
we have in the National Gallery *Portraits of Jean Arnolfini and
his Wife*, a picture which is a masterpiece of colour, and light, and
shade, combining these qualities with an inconceivable minuteness and finish of execution ; it bears the inscription, as though
written on the walls of the room, JOHANNES DE EYCK FUIT HIC,
1434.   Two other pictures by this master are in the National
Gallery.   A portrait of a man in a turban, believed to be a
likeness of the painter himself, and a portrait of a man in a
dark red dress and a green hood.   There are also some good
specimens of Jan van Eyck's pictures in the possession of
private collectors in England.

We owe to the brothers Van Eyck the substitution of the
picture, in the place of wall-painting and illumination.   Henceforth pictures were to be carried about, and their beauties
extended to many lands, instead of remaining fixed upon a
particular spot, just as the illuminated manuscript, securely kept
in one position, was to give place to the printed book, copies of
which were scattered far and wide.   Of the works of Lambert

* Als ich kan—the first words of an old Flemish proverb, " As I can,
but not as I will."

and Margaretha van Eyck, brother and sister of the famous master, no authentic records remain.

Although the School of Bruges began, grew, and reached its highest point during the lives of its founders, the brothers Van Eyck, and although none of the scholars of those masters ever excelled their teachers, yet we find several painters of note who adopted the newly-discovered process of painting in oils. The secret of that process, though jealously guarded by the Flemish Guilds, was carried as far as Italy, and was very popular in Venice. One great result of this discovery was, that Art ceased to be exclusively the handmaid of Religion; and in the future, instead of decorating the walls of churches with scenes from Holy Writ, or ecclesiastical tradition, artists painted pictures of everyday life, often, as in the case of the Dutch artists, selecting subjects of the most coarse and vulgar character.

Of the followers of the Van Eycks we must briefly mention the following painters:

PETRUS CRISTUS, who was born at Baerle, near Deynze, studied under Jan van Eyck. Possibly he was a student of the works of both brothers, as his pictures resemble Huibrecht rather than Jan. His chief works are a *Virgin and Saints* (1447), in the Städel Institute, Frankfort; a *Last Judgment* (1452), in the Berlin Museum; a *Crucifixion*, in the Hermitage, St. Petersburg; and the *St. Elisius* in the Oppenheim collection at Cologne. A *Portrait of Marco Barbarigo*, in the National Gallery, usually attributed to Gerard van der Meire, is assigned by Mr. J. A. Crowe to Petrus Cristus, whom he declares to be the only direct disciple of the great master of Bruges. Petrus Cristus purchased the freedom of Bruges in 1444, was free of the guild in 1450, and was still living in that city in 1471.

HUGO VAN DER GOES is known by only one authentic picture, though he must have executed many works in the course of a long and laborious life. Of that life little is known with certainty. He lived in Ghent, his native city, for a long period,

GFDP   F

but Van Mander describes him as a painter of Bruges. The same
writer calls him a pupil of Jan van Eyck, but the one picture by
which he is known, *The Nativity*, in Santa Maria Nuova at
Florence, owes little or nothing to the teaching of Van Eyck. We
know that in 1468 Van der Goes was employed to prepare devices
and ornaments for the pageants which adorned the marriage of
Charles the Bold and Margaret of York ; but he could do far
better work than the production of whales which spouted up
mermaids, and mysterious pasties full of musicians. We find
him presiding as Elder of the Guild of Ghent in 1472, but in
1476 he had entered the monastery of Rooden Cloestere, near
Brussels. Van der Goes, however, brought great scandal on the
monastery by his drunken revels, and was expelled. His end
was sad enough ; he went mad, and died in 1482, his insanity
having partially disappeared. He is described by Mr. J. A.
Crowe as " the earliest master of this school who painted blue
draperies, broken with green, combining further with this mixture
an orange colour, which is far from enhancing the general harmony. In other respects he possesses the highest qualities of the
Flemish school. His portraits are true to nature and animated,
his drawing is good and conscientiously carried out in every
part, and his execution is solid." The *Nativity* still remains
in excellent preservation in the Church of Santa Maria Nuova
at Florence, but is removed from its original place on the
altar.

GERARD VAN DER MEIRE lived at Ghent in the second half of
the fifteenth century, and was free of the Painters' Guild in 1452.
Many pictures at Berlin and other galleries are attributed to him,
but only one work can be assigned to him with certainty ; this
is a triptych in a chapel at St. Bavon at Ghent, representing *The
Crucifixion ; The Lifting up of the Brazen Serpent ;* and *Moses
Striking the Rock.* If the pictures attributed to Van der Meire
are really his, he was more a follower of Van der Weyden than
of Van Eyck.

Justus, or Jodocus, van Ghent, transported the lessons which he had learned from the Van Eycks to Italy. He was formerly confounded with another painter called Justus d'Alemanno, the author of an *Annunciation* in Santa Maria di Castello, date 1451, but later critics have discovered the mistake. Justus van Ghent painted, in 1468-70, *The Last Supper*, an altar-piece for Sant' Agatha at Urbino. It was executed for the brotherhood of Corpus Christi, and paid for by the liberality of Federigo di Montefeltro, Duke of Urbino, and others. The portraits of the Duke and of Caterino Zeno, Envoy of Venice, appear in the picture. It is probable that Justus van Ghent also painted the series of *Poets, Philosophers*, and *Doctors of the Church* to adorn the library of Duke Federigo at Urbino. In this work the painter shows the influence of Italian Masters, acting upon his own native style. His great fault is in his perspective.

Rogier van der Weyden was formerly considered as a pupil of Jan van Eyck. It is now, however, satisfactorily proved that he was the rival, not the scholar, of that master, and that the school which originated in the valley of the Schelde, exercised a greater influence over the later art of Germany and the Netherlands than that of the Van Eycks in the valley of the Maes. Van der Weyden was born at Tournai, in 1399 (or 1400), an ancient and important city, and famous for its tinted sculpture. It is believed that this master himself practised the art of tinting statues, and the influence of coloured sculpture is clearly traceable in his pictures. Instead of being apprenticed to Jan van Eyck, as was formerly supposed, Van der Weyden became the pupil of an unknown master, one Robert Campin, in 1426 and ten years later had attained the dignity of town painter of Brussels. In 1449 he went to Italy, and probably taught the Flemish method of oil painting to the Italians. He was in Rome at the year of Jubilee, 1450, and returned to his home in the same year. Van der Weyden was one of the first of his brethren to visit Italy, but, unlike so many of his successors, he retained his originality. He died in 1464, and was buried at Brussels " under a blue stone, before St. Catharine's altar " in the Church of St. Gudule. Van der Weyden chose to describe the darker and more sombre side of religious art; the Church militant, with its martyrs in their agony, was more pleasing to his eyes than the glories of the Church triumphant; and the story of Jesus, the Man of Sorrows, interested him more than the smiling Virgin and happy faces of the infant Christ, which others delighted to portray. The earlier pictures of this master are entirely lost. His master-piece is the *Last Judgment*, painted in 1443 for the hospital of Chancellor Rollin at Beaune. It is an altar-piece representing Christ in the centre seated on a rainbow, His feet resting on the earth. Beneath Him is the Archangel Michael weighing the souls of men in a balance. The side panels depict the resurrection of the Just and the Lost, the fate of the latter being described with the realistic force which is the great characteristic of this master. The outer panels of the picture contain figures of *St. Sebastian* and *St. Anthony*, and the figures of the *Chancellor Rollin* and *His wife*. St. Anthony is said to be " one of the noblest creations of the Flemish School " (Crowe and Cavalcaselle).

Another famous picture by Van der Weyden is an *Adoration of the Kings*, in the Munich Gallery, containing, under the guise of the foremost of the kings, a portrait of Philippe le Bon of Burgundy (Fig. 31). The picture of *St. Luke painting the Virgin*, also in the Munich Gallery, was long attributed to Jan van Eyck—the distant landscape indeed recalls the work of the master of Bruges, especially the *Madonna* in the Louvre. The picture is, however, undoubtedly by Van der Weyden. In the Berlin Museum there is amongst others an altar-piece by this master, representing three scenes from the *Life of St. John the Baptist*. England possesses in the National Gallery an *Entombment of Christ*, by Van der Weyden, full of pathos, and with an

exquisitely painted landscape background of a stream running
through wooded hills and fields. It is painted in tempera upon
linen. The pictures of Rogier van der Weyden, like those of the
Van Eycks and of the Flemish School of this period generally,
are frequently characterized by the profuse introduction of architecture of a fanciful Gothic type, which by its detail gives great
richness to the general effect; while the long straight lines of the
slender columns and mouldings, and the delicate greys of the
stone-work, are of the greatest value as a setting to the colour of
the flesh and the brilliant richness of the draperies. A picture
of the *Seven Sacraments* at Antwerp, attributed to Van der
Weyden, is a remarkable and elaborate instance of this manner
of treatment. He is said to have been the first artist who
painted on fixed canvas instead of on panels. It is to him
that we owe the spread of the realistic tendencies of the Van
Eycks throughout Germany. Martin Schongauer was, as we
have seen, his pupil.

The greatest of Van der Weyden's scholars was HANS MEMLING,
formerly called Memlinc, or Memlinghe, and from a mistake in
the first letter, Hemling. Divested of romance, the record of
Memling's life is very meagre. The romance, however, is interesting, though untrustworthy. It tells us how, after the fatal
fight at Nancy, where Charles the Bold fought his last battle, a
man of middle age, evidently a soldier, arrived wounded and
fainting at the Hospital of St. John at Bruges. After being
kindly cared for, he recovered and told his deliverers that he
had been a painter before becoming a soldier. Calling for
painting materials, he painted the *Sibyl Zambeth* on the walls
of the Hospital, and executed other works in token of his grati-
tude. Stern fact and cold criticism have dissipated this pleasing
romance of Hans Memling's life. Memling was a quiet citizen of
Bruges, where he died in 1495; and though some of his most
famous pictures are in the Hospital of St. John, there is no reason
to suppose that he was ever a soldier, or shared the misfortunes

FIG. 32.—PORTRAIT OF MARTIN VAN NEWENHOWEN. BY MEMLING.
Part of a Diptych, in the Hospital of St. John, Bruges.

of Charles the Bold at Nancy. One of his finest works is a large altar-piece of the *Last Judgment*, commissioned for Italy, and painted about the year 1470. This picture was taken at sea by a pirate of Dantzic, and is now in the cathedral there. In the Hospital of St. John is the beautiful triptych of the *Marriage of St. Catharine*, probably finished in 1479. The Virgin is seated under a porch, with tapestry at the back. Two angels are holding a crown above her head; and the head of the kneeling St. Catharine is one of the finest of Memling's creations. The whole work may be considered as his masterpiece. Another triptych, painted in the same year, depicts the *Adoration of the Magi* in the centre, the *Nativity* on the left hand, and the *Presentation in the Temple* on the right hand. From the inscription written on it in Flemish, we learn that Memling painted the picture for Jan Floreins (alias Van der Riist), brother of St. John's Hospital, in 1479. In the same building is a diptych, containing a beautifully-painted *Virgin and Holy Child*, with a portrait of the donor, *Martin van Newenhoven* (Fig. 32), on the other side.

But the most famous work by this master in the Hospital of St. John is the *Reliquary of St. Ursula* (Fig. 33). The Reliquary is a small ark, formed like a Gothic chapel, and intended of course to contain relics : Memling's pictures form, so to speak, frescoes for this miniature temple. At one end is painted the *Madonna*, at the other *St. Ursula* holding an arrow, the instrument of her martyrdom. Under her robes are the ten virgins, St. Ursula forming the eleventh. The common legend of the eleven *thousand* virgins originated in the mistake of a chronicler of the Middle Ages. There are three medallions on each of the sloping parts of the roof of this reliquary, representing St. Ursula leading her companions to martyrdom, and crowned with glory in the presence of the Blessed Trinity. The sides of the reliquary contain miniature paintings, describing the whole story of St. Ursula and her virgins, from their

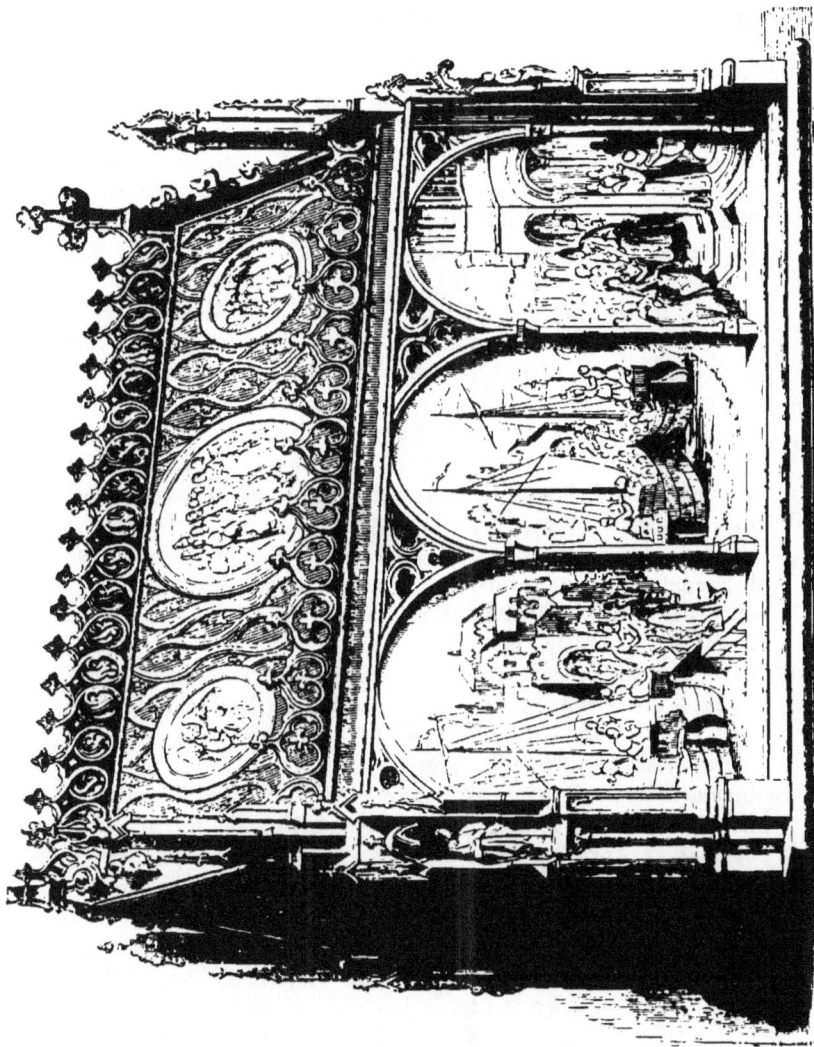

FIG. 33.—THE RELIQUARY OF ST. URSULA. BY MEMLING.

In the Hospital of St. John, Bruge•

departure from Cologne to their return to that city, and
their martyrdom at the hands of the Huns.   The beauty
of the virgin martyrs suggests that Memling was not un-
observant of the fair faces of Bruges, which was famed for its
lovely women,—"*formosis Bruga puellis.*" ⤭ The pictures in
the *Reliquary of St. Ursula* are overcrowded with figures and
incidents, a fault common to all the works of Memling; this
is especially noticeable in the picture of *The Seven Joys of the
Virgin* in the Munich Gallery.   The faults of Memling, however, are very few; his faces are characterized by some of the
asceticism of his master, but tempered with sweetness, and his
pictures are full of a devout and reverential feeling. As a
colourist he is perhaps even more remarkable than Van Eyck
or Van der Weyden; there is in the colours of his draperies
a purity and brilliant depth of tint which makes them glow
like the heart of a gem; and he was also well aware of the
value of architecture in his compositions.   His landscape
backgrounds are crowded with minute detail, executed with
exquisite finish and atmospheric transparency.   The execution
is no less complete than with either of these masters, though
never perhaps carried to the marvellous minuteness of Jan van
Eyck. ⤭There is one of his paintings in the National Gallery,
the *Virgin and Child enthroned in a Garden.*   Besides these
pictures, Memling is well known by the miniatures in the celebrated Grimani Breviary at Venice.   After Memling's death the
School of Bruges ceased to be representative, and the influence
of that of Antwerp asserted itself.   Before we pass, however,
to Antwerp, we must notice very briefly three other painters.

DIERIC BOUTS, formerly called erroneously STUERBOUT, was
born at Haarlem, probably in 1391.   Though a Dutchman by
birth, he is entirely a painter of the Flemish School of Van
Eyck.   He was town-painter at Louvain in 1461, and held that
office till his death in 1475.   His two greatest works are
pictures painted for the council-chamber of the town-hall at

FIG. 34.—THE LAST SUPPER. BY DIERIC BOUTS.
In St. Peter's, at Louvain.

Louvain in 1468. They represent the *Triumph of Justice*, as exhibited in the legend of Otho III., who having executed a guiltless courtier on the testimony of a false woman, discovers the truth, and commits the accuser, his own wife, to the flames. In St. Peter's, at Louvain, there is a *Last Supper* by him (Fig. 34), showing a very unusual treatment of the subject. There is in the National Gallery *The Exhumation of St. Hubert*, attributed to Dierick Bouts, but its authorship is uncertain. On the other hand, the *Portrait of a Man*, there "ascribed to Memling," is given by some critics to Bouts.

ROGIER VAN DER WEYDEN "the younger" was born about 1450. He was a son and pupil of the elder painter of the same name. We know nothing of his life except that he made considerable sums of money by his pictures, and was very liberal in his gifts. He was made Master of the Guild of Painters at Antwerp in 1528, and died in that town in the following year. Many pictures attributed to this master are to be found in Madrid, Berlin, Naples, London, and elsewhere, but they are all of doubtful authorship. In the National Gallery are four very pleasing pictures which *may* have been painted by Van der Weyden the younger—they are *Portraits of Himself and his Wife*, a *Magdalen*, a *Mater Dolorosa*, and an *Ecce Homo*.

Besides the painters here mentioned, are numerous followers of these masters, known and unknown, and frequently producing works of very high excellence. Their pictures abound in the galleries of Belgium and elsewhere, notably at Madrid, and so closely resemble each other that it is most difficult to assign even the best of them to the right authors.

Of those in the National Gallery may be mentioned a picture by Gheerardt David, representing a *Canon of St. Donatian with his Patron Saints*, remarkable for the elaborate rendering of the magnificent brocaded copes and other rich vestments, no less than for the fine character of the heads; also an *Entombment* by an unknown artist of the School of Van der Weyden, beautiful in sentiment and in colour.

GHEERARDT DAVID (son of Jan, son of David) was born at
Oudewater about the middle of the fifteenth century; he pro-
bably learnt his art in Holland, and settled in Bruges towards
the close of 1483, and acquired the right of citizenship, taking
" David" for his surname. In 1484 he was made free of the
Painters' Guild, and in 1501-2 he served as Dean. He was well
employed in Bruges, and on his death in 1523, was buried in
Notre Dame, in that city. His best works, in the Museum of
Bruges, are the *Judgment of Cambyses*, and the *Flaying of
Sisannes*, completed for the Hall of Justice, in 1498; the *Bap-
tism of Christ*, of the year 1507; and the picture, mentioned
above, in the National Gallery.

The works of the Flemish painters of this period, though not
less devout in feeling than those of the early Italian School, differ
from them completely in the elaborate realism of the treatment.
The simple, broadly-painted figures on gold grounds of the
Florentines and Sienese are unknown to the Flemish painters,
who crowded their back-grounds with minute details of architecture and landscape, and other rich accessories, painted with
an exquisite purity of tint and a perfection of finish which
has never been equalled in any other school or at any other
time On these points the Flemish painters as far excel the
Italians as the latter are superior to them in the grandeur
and simplicity of style which they gained from their practice
in wall-decoration. Mantegna or Antonello da Messina may
be said, perhaps, to have rivalled them on the point of finished
execution, and the early Venetians excel them, if not in the
harmonious combinations of their colours, yet certainly in the
luminous glow in which their pictures seem to be steeped; but
the extraordinary clearness and brilliancy of colour in the works
of Flemish artists, due to the care and patience with which they
prepared and used their pigments, and the marvellous perfection
of the workmanship, added to their other high artistic qualities,
gives a special and exceptional interest to the study of this
school.

CHAPTER II.

ANTWERP at the beginning of the sixteenth century occupied the first place as a School of Art in the Netherlands. The founder of this School was QUINTEN MASSIJS (1466—1531*), usually called MATSYS, and sometimes METSYS : he is popularly known as "the Blacksmith of Antwerp." Born at Louvain, the son of a locksmith, Quinten Matsys probably worked at first at his father's trade; but the iron tracery representing vine leaves, which is preserved in Antwerp and Louvain as the early work of Quinten, was probably executed by his elder brother, who followed the calling of his father. Every one knows the story of Quinten Matsys's love which led him to leave the anvil for the paint-brush. The father of his lady-love had declared that she should marry a painter, and Quinten Matsys accordingly studied art, probably with Dieric Bouts. There seems to be no reason for disbelieving this pretty romance; in the Latin inscription in honour of Matsys in Antwerp Cathedral occurs the line—" *Connubialis amor de*

---

* The dates 1529 and 1530 are also given.

Mulcibre fecit Apellem," and the master himself wrote on his
own portrait the words, "*Pictorem me fecit Amor.*" In 1497
Quinten Matsys settled at Antwerp, and joined the Painters'
Guild. He rapidly became famous. In 1508, he painted his
masterpiece, *The Entombment,* executed as an altar-piece for the
chapel of the Joiners' Company in Antwerp Cathedral, and now
in the Museum at Antwerp (Fig. 35). It is a triptych, representing
in the centre the dead body of Christ after the descent from the
cross, the holy women and others mourning over it. The right
wing depicts the head of St. John the Baptist placed on the table
of Herod; on the left wing is St. John the Evangelist in the
cauldron of boiling oil. Sir Joshua Reynolds says of this work :
"There are heads in this picture not exceeded by Raphael, and
indeed not unlike his manner of painting portraits, hard and
minutely finished. The head of Herod, and of a fat man near
the Christ, are excellent." For this wonderful picture, which
unites the vigorous colouring of the Van Eycks with the noble
simplicity of Memling, the elaborate finish of Denner, and the
grandeur of Rubens, Matsys received only 300 florins (about
£25), and we find that even that paltry amount was not paid at
once. Philip II. of Spain, and Elizabeth of England, offered
large sums for the *Entombment,* in vain. It was sold, however,
in 1580 to the magistrates of Antwerp for 1500 florins. Matsys
forms the connecting link between the old and the new styles of
art, and unites both in his pictures. The religious fervour of
the Middle Ages, and the realism, often coarse and grotesque, of
later schools, find expression in the style of the Antwerp painter.
The realistic side is shown in the various *Money-pieces* which
Matsys has given us. Many of those attributed to him are
probably the work of his son, and other copyists; the famous
picture of the *Misers,* at Windsor Castle, is said by Dr. Waagen
to be a copy ; another picture of the same subject in the National
Gallery, formerly given to Matsys, is now more properly attributed
to MARINUS DE SEEUW, or ZEEUW, who painted between 1521 and

FIG. 36.—THE BANKER AND HIS WIFE. BY MATSYS.
In the Louvre, Paris

1541); but he is represented there by a diptych containing
heads of the *Saviour and the Virgin*. In the Louvre we have
a genuine work in *The Banker and his Wife*, signed by Quinten
Matsys, and bearing the date 1518 (Fig. 36). Matsys was twice
married, and died at Antwerp in 1531, leaving a large family:
two of his sons were painters. Portraits of Matsys and his second
wife are in the Uffizi Gallery.

We have traced the decadence of German Art from the death
of Albrecht Dürer. From the death of his contemporary
Quinten Matsys we may trace the gradual decline of art in the
Netherlands. The manly, robust, and realistic style of the
Flemish painters, which had helped to form the art of Martin
Schongauer and others of the German School, was now to be
abandoned for the dreams and idealism of Italy. Flemish art
ceased to be national, and its painters forsook the delineation of
their own homely people, their quaint old-world cities, and their
flat landscapes, to struggle after the azure skies and unveiled
beauties of the Florentine and Venetian Schools. The realistic
character of the Fleming was as out of place in ideal Italy as a
Byzantine palace on a Yorkshire moor, and so we find a gradual
and marked decadence in the art of the Low Countries, happily
arrested by the revival under Rubens.

One of the first to feel the effect of the Italian Renaissance,
although he must not be classed with Flemish "Italianisers,"
was JAN GOSSART,* commonly called MABUSE (about 1470—
1532). His more generally-known name of Mabuse is derived
from his birthplace, Maubeuge: and hence he frequently signed
himself " Malbodius." We do not know much of the incidents
of his life. He entered the Guild of Antwerp in 1503. He
probably studied in the School of Quinten Matsys, and as
long as he painted in the Flemish style he equalled that
master in power of colour and execution. Mabuse, however,
went to Italy in 1513 with his patron Philippe of Bur-

* Often written Gossaert.

FIG. 37.—ST. LUKE PAINTING THE VIRGIN. BY MABUSE.
In the Cathedral at Prague.

gundy, Bishop and Admiral, and soon forsook his national
art to copy Michelangelo and Leonardo da Vinci. After the
death of Philippe of Burgundy, the Marquis Van Veeren became
the patron of Mabuse. Tradition tells us that the painter was
fonder of the wine-cup than of his work, and a story is related
of him which, if doubtful, is at least amusing. The Emperor
Charles V. was on one occasion coming on a visit to the Marquis
Van Veeren, and in honour of the guest all the members of the
household were to be dressed in white damask. Mabuse got
possession of his costly garment and sold it, spending the pro-
ceeds in a tavern. On the arrival of the emperor, however, the
painter appeared in a white dress which outshone in splendour
those of his companions, and Charles V. was not a little amused
when, on examining the gorgeous robe, he discovered that it
consisted of paper, painted by Mabuse to imitate damask. Van
Mander believes that Mabuse visited England, but no record of
his stay there remains. We know, however, that he painted
pictures for Christian II., King of Denmark, and for Margaret of
Austria. He died at Antwerp in 1532, but not in prison, as some
of his biographers have stated.

Mabuse was the first painter of his country to introduce
the composite style of Italianized Flemish art which marks this
epoch of painting in the Netherlands. His works are numerous,
and may be found in Antwerp, Brussels, Munich, Berlin,
St. Petersburg, Paris, and at Hampton Court. In the Antwerp
Museum we see Mabuse in his Flemish style illustrated in the
Four Maries returning from the Tomb of Christ, and in the
Upright Judges. In the Berlin Gallery two diptychs display the composite art—half Flemish, half Italian—of Mabuse.
They represent *Adam and Eve*, and *Neptune and Amphitrite*,
the latter is signed by the painter—" Joannes Malbodius pinge-
bat, 1516." This date shows that the pictures were painted
after Mabuse had visited Italy. In England there are two
good specimens of his earlier and better style, the *Adoration*

of the Kings, at Castle Howard; and the *Children of Christian II.,* at Hampton Court. He also was fond of introducing a profusion of architectural details into his pictures, as in his *St. Luke painting the Virgin,* at Prague (Fig. 37), but with him the elegant Gothic of the Van Eycks and Van der Weyden has become a clumsy form of the Classic Renaissance.

BAREND * VAN ORLEY was born at Brussels between 1488 and 1490. In 1518 he was appointed painter to Margaret of Austria. Nine years later he was convicted of heresy and deprived of his post, but in 1532 he was re-instated by Mary of Hungary. He died at Brussels in 1542. That he visited Italy is apparent; but the statement that he there studied under Raphael and subsequently assisted Van Coxcien to superintend at Arras the manufacture of the tapestry designed by Raphael is open to question. Van Orley seems to have been a prosperous man. Dürer met him at Brussels, and mentions that, "Meister Bernhart gave him so costly a meal that it could not be paid for with ten florins." Van Orley entirely forsook the art of his country, and strove after Raphael, but with feeble success. His colouring is cold, though gaudy, and his religious pictures have little or no religion in them. At the Church of Our Lady at Lübeck is a polyptych by Van Orley — the centre depicts the *Trinity adored by Saints;* on the wings we find the *Annunciation,* the *Sibyl and Augustus, St. John the Evangelist,* and the *Four Latin Fathers.* In the National Gallery is a *Magdalen reading,* by this painter.

MICHIEL VAN COXCIEN,† who was born at Mechlin in 1499, was a pupil first of his father, an unimportant painter, and then of Van Orley. He has been styled "the Flemish

* Or Bernaerd : but more frequently written Bernhard.

† His name is found written in a variety of ways : *e.g.* Coxie, Coxcie, Cocxie, Coxis, and Coxcyen. A *Martyrdom of St. Sebastian* in the metropolitan church at Mechlin bears his signature MICHAEL D. COXCIEN ; and another *Martyrdom of St. Sebastian* in the Antwerp Gallery is signed MICHIEL D. COXCYEN,

Raphael," but his pictures are remarkable chiefly as exhibiting the decline of national art in the Low Countries. In the Antwerp Museum there is *a Martyrdom of St. Sebastian* by his hand, but his best work is a copy of Van Eyck's *Adoration of the Mystic Lamb*, painted for his patron, Philip II. Part of this picture is in the Berlin Museum, part in the Munich Gallery. Van Coxcien died at Mechlin in 1592.

JAN VAN SCHOREEL*—or more correctly Schoorl, his birthplace, near Alkmaar—(1495—1562), studied under Mabuse, and also, it is said, under Albrecht Dürer. Although a painter of a higher order than Van Orley or Coxcien, there is little which is original or pleasing in his composite Germanized-Italian-Flemish style. Had he not gone to Rome, and lost all love of natural art, he might have been a great painter. In the National Gallery there is a picture, *The Repose in Egypt*, with St. Joseph offering a plate of fruit to the Saviour, which is attributed to Schoreel. His earlier works, in which the German style predominates, are often attributed to Dürer. Schoreel, who died a Prebendary of the Church of St. Mary at Utrecht, is said to have been an accomplished linguist, poet, and musician.

LAMBERT LOMBARD (wrongly called SUAVIUS or SUSTERMAN),† who was born at Liege in 1506, formed his style under the influence of Mabuse at Middelburg, and visited Italy in the train of Cardinal Pole. Later he established a school in his native city, which was numerously attended by students, and thus the number of the *Italianizers* was greatly multiplied. He died at Liege in 1566. Lombard's best works are the *Pestilence*, and *Shipwreck*, in the King of Holland's gallery. There is a picture by Lombard, *The taking down from the Cross*, in the National Gallery.

Another of these degenerate Flemings is FRANS DE VRIENDT, called commonly FRANS FLORIS, a pupil of Lombard at Liege.

* The *ch* in Dutch and Flemish is always pronounced hard, like the English *k*, or the Greek χ.

† See Catalogue of the Berlin Gallery, by Dr. Julius Meyer and Dr. Wilhelm Bode, 1878.

He was born at Antwerp, about 1520; the son of a stonemason, he at first turned his attention to sculpture, which he afterwards forsook for painting. After going to Italy, like the rest of his brethren, he founded a school at Antwerp which was said to have been attended by one hundred and twenty scholars, of which no less than twenty-six are mentioned, by name, by Van Mander; but curiously enough not one of these was ever registered in the Guild of St. Luke at Antwerp as a pupil of De Vriendt. He was a painter of considerable genius, but unfortunately he diverted that genius into the wrong channel. He seems to have made much money by his painting, and built himself a splendid house in Antwerp, where he died, some say, from excessive drinking, in 1570. His three best works are in the Antwerp Gallery—they are *The Fall of the Angels*, *The Adoration of the Shepherds*, and *St. Luke Painting the Virgin*.

There is little profit in tracing the Italianizers step by step in their downward course. Somewhat better than the crowd of copyists are the three Brueghels,* known from the subjects of their pictures as "Peasant † Brueghel," "Hell ‡ Brueghel," and "Velvet § Brueghel." PIETER BRUEGHEL, or "the Peasant," was born at the village of Brueghel, near Breda, about 1520. He went to Italy as a matter of course. His favourite scenes are taken from peasant life, and he is said to have joined in many a rustic revel disguised in a peasant's clothes. There is a coarse humour about his pictures, which, if vulgar, is better than the insipid productions of his contemporaries. His best works are in the Vienna Gallery. He died at Brussels in 1569.

---

* The name of this family of painters is derived from the village of Brueghel (or Bruegel), near Breda—the birthplace of the eldest member. It was adopted by him, and became to all intents and purposes a surname.

The modern form of writing the name of this village is Breughel, or Breugel; hence the fact that the name of the painters is often so written. But the way they themselves write it, and consequently the *right* way, is Brueghel, or sometimes Bruegel.

† Bauern.　　　　‡ Höllen.　　　　§ Fluweelen.

PIETER BRUEGHEL, the younger, or "Hell" Brueghel, born at Brussels in 1564, is inferior to his father. *The Alchemist*, now in private possession at Antwerp (Fig. 39), is very characteristic of his very peculiar style. His best work is *Christ bearing the Cross*, in the Antwerp Museum. He died in 1637, at Antwerp.

JAN BRUEGHEL, or "Velvet" Brueghel (born about 1589, died about 1642), is, on the other hand, decidedly superior to his

FIG. 38.—RIVER SCENE. BY JAN BRUEGHEL.

father. He painted landscapes as backgrounds for many artists, including Rubens. In pictures of peasant life, and scenes of fantastic demonology, he is excellent. Good specimens of his works are in the galleries of Dresden, Berlin, and Madrid, and in the Louvre. In the Hague Gallery is one of the best of his landscapes, the figures of Adam and Eve being by Rubens.

The portrait painters of his time occupy deservedly a higher place than the Italian copyists.

Sir ANTONIS MOR (usually written MORO, occasionally MOOR), was born at Utrecht in 1512, but though a Dutchman by birth he studied art in Flanders. He visited Italy, but escaped the prevailing epidemic of plagiarism, and on his return studied the works of Hans Holbein. Charles V. employed Mor to paint the portrait of Queen Mary of England, to whom Philip II. was betrothed. That unhappy Princess retained the painter at her court at a salary of £100 a year. Mor was highly esteemed in England as a portrait painter, and was well paid for his work. He returned to Madrid on the death of Queen Mary and painted for Philip II. In 1560 he left the court in disgrace; perhaps, as one story has it, because he returned, with his maulstick, a blow given him by the king. In this year (1560) he took the freedom of the Guild at Antwerp. Later we find Philip vainly trying to induce Mor to return. In the Netherlands he found a patron in the Duke of Alva, who made him Receiver-General of the Revenues of West Flanders. Mor died between 1576 and 1578 at Antwerp, whither he had gone in 1572. It is not known where or by whom he was knighted. In England we have by his hand a *Portrait of Queen Mary*, belonging to Lord Yarborough, and a *Portrait of Jeanne d'Archel* in the National Gallery. The Madrid Museum contains many of his portraits, but in none does he equal Holbein.

It was at this period that landscape painting flourished, for its own sake, and not merely for the sake of background. The earliest master of any school to devote himself to landscape in its true character was JOACHIM DE PATINIR,* born at Dinant at the end of the fifteenth century. The dates of his birth and death are uncertain. He was admitted as a master in the Guild of St. Luke at Antwerp in 1515; and was dead in 1524. Patinir was twice married, and at his second wedding Albrecht Dürer was present and drew his portrait. It was in the later years of his life that Patinir devoted himself to landscape painting; in

* Or Patenier.

FIG. 40.—PORTRAIT OF SIR ANTONIS MOR. BY HIMSELF.

his earlier days he showed himself a fair historical painter. There are six of his pictures at Madrid, the *Temptation of St. Anthony* being a really fine work, with a highly poetical landscape and much character in the heads; and four in the National Gallery, of which *St. Christopher* is the best example of his style.   He had a faithful follower in HERRI BLES,* who was called by the Italians CIVETTA, from his monogram of an owl.   At Munich there is an *Adoration of the Kings* † by his hand, and in the National Gallery we find a *Christ on the Cross,* and a *Magdalen.*   Bles was born at Bouvignes, near Namur, in 1480; and died after 1521, probably at Liege.

The best of the Flemish landscape painters was PAUWEL (generally known as PAUL) BRIL.   He was born at Antwerp in 1556, and studied in Rome under his elder brother Matthäus, whose early death deprived the world of many good pictures.   On the death of his brother, Paul Bril received from the Pope the same pension which Matthäus had enjoyed. For his patron, Pope Sixtus V., Bril painted several works in the Sistine Chapel, in Santa Maria Maggiore, and in San Giovanni in Laterano.   He painted in oil and fresco. Kugler says of him : " He viewed nature with a fresh eye— selecting her natural and poetic rather than her arbitrary and fantastic features.   He was the first to introduce a certain unity of light in his pictures, attaining thereby a far finer general effect than those who had preceded him.   His deficiencies lie in the overforce, and also in the monotonous green, of his foregrounds, and in the exaggerated blueness of his distances." ‡ There are good specimens of Paul Bril's pictures in the Louvre and the Berlin Museum.   Annibale Carracci not infrequently assisted him by adding the groups of figures to his landscapes.

* He is usually called Herri met de Bles (Henry with the forelock) ; but this is now thought to be an error.

† This work is signed HENRICUS BLESIUS F. ; but Mr. J. A. Crowe considers that the signature is " probably a forgery."

‡ 'Handbook of Painting.   The German, Flemish, and Dutch Schools. Based on the Handbook of Kugler.'   By J. A. Crowe.   1874.

FIG. 41.—DUCK-SHOOTING. BY PAUL BRIL.

CHAPTER III.

(1600—1700.)

THE commencement of the seventeenth century witnessed the return of art in the Netherlands to the honest realism of the North, after its long banishment amid the idealism of the South.   Probably the Venetian School of Painting at this period exercised as great an influence for good on Flemish art as the Schools of Rome and Florence had done for evil.   It required, however, a potent magician to recall the Art of the Netherlands to life, and that magician appeared in the person of PETER PAUL RUBENS.   Few men have led more stirring and successful lives.   No painter except Titian was ever so courted by the great and wealthy.   Handsome, well-born, fascinating in manner, Rubens succeeded in all which he undertook, and was equally praised as a diplomatist, a courtier, a patron, and a painter.   He was essentially a man of the world, and born under a lucky star.   His very pictures may be described as worldly, since though by no means irreligious as a man, there is no religion, no *spirituality*, in his works.   Ruskin has described him "as a healthy, worthy, kind-hearted, courtly-phrased animal, without any clearly percept ble traces of a soul."   The last phrase, if applied to *his works*, is not unfairly descriptive; but it seems rather hard to accuse the poor man himself of having no soul, because his nature led him to an impetuous display of his great technical powers. A more correct description of him would be that his exuberant facility was not corrected by refinement nor exalted by imagination, so that his works frequently are coarse and tainted with vulgarity, especially when he treats religious subjects. But this is not the case with his portraits, which are often full of dignity and even grandeur.

Rubens was born on the day of the festival of St. Peter and St. Paul—the 29th of June, 1577, at Siegen* in Westphalia. His father was a physician, who being suspected of Protestant proclivities had been forced to flee from his native town of Antwerp, and was subsequently imprisoned, not without cause, by William of Orange, whose side he had joined. When Peter Paul was a year old, his parents removed to Cologne, where they remained for nine years, and then on the death of her husband, the mother of Rubens returned with her child to Antwerp. Young Rubens was sent to a Jesuit school, doubtless in proof of his mother's soundness in the faith of Rome, and studied art under Tobias Verhaeght, Adam van Noort, and Othon van Veen, generally called Otto Venius. Fortunately for the world, Rubens possessed too original a genius to be much influenced by these masters. He visited Italy in 1600, where the colouring of the Venetians exercised a great influence upon the young painter, and we may consider Paolo Veronese as the source of inspiration from which Rubens derived the richness of his tints.   In 1601 we find Rubens in the service of Duke Vincenzo Gonzaga of Mantua, an enthusiastic patron of art,

* The birthplace of this great painter has been the subject of endless controversy. Cologne, Siegen, and Antwerp have all striven for the honour. Cologne is now dismissed from the argument. The greatest weight of evidence seems in favour of Siegen, yet the claims of Antwerp are still supported by some writers.

and two years later he was sent to Philip III. of Spain on an
"artistic commission," some secret mission perhaps, but certainly
as the bearer of costly presents.   On his return from Spain
he passed some time in Mantua, Rome, and Genoa; the *dramatic
power* of his pictures he derived probably from Michelangelo, as
he had learned richness of colouring from Veronese, and we can
trace the influence of Giulio Romano, whose works he must have
studied at Mantua.   Numberless sketches from statues and pictures in Italy are a proof of the eagerness with which he studied
all forms of fine art which came under his notice on his travels.
In the National Gallery, for instance, is a large oil-sketch from a
portion of the *Triumph of Cæsar*, by Mantegna, now at Hampton
Court, with a back-ground of his own composition; and his
drawing in the Louvre, from the celebrated cartoon by Leonardo
da Vinci, is well known, and is the only remaining record of
that work.*

In 1608, Rubens hastily returned to Antwerp, summoned by
the illness of his mother, whom he never saw again in life.
Intending to return to Mantua, he yielded to the persuasion of
the Archduke Albert, and remained in the Netherlands; and in
1609 he was appointed court-painter to the Archduke and his
Duchess Isabella.   Rubens settled in Antwerp, and married in
1609 his first wife, Isabella Brandt.   Always popular, and always
successful, Rubens founded a School of painting in Antwerp,
which was soon crowded with pupils.   His life, however, was
destined to be full of action and movement.   In 1620 he went
to Paris at the invitation of Marie de Medicis, then living in the
Luxembourg Palace.   The work which the widowed Queen
proposed to Rubens was to decorate two galleries, the one with
scenes from her own history, the other with pictures from the
life of Henri IV.   In 1621 Rubens was painting the sketches
for the first series of pictures under the eyes of Marie de
Medicis; these sketches were elaborated in the studio at Antwerp,

* See the *Text-book of Classic and Italian Painters.*

by the master and his pupils, and were finished in 1625. The story of Henri IV.'s life was cut short by the exile of the Queen.

In 1626, Rubens visited Holland, saw the principal painters of that country, and lost his wife in the same year. The picture of the two sons of this marriage is in the Lichtenstein Gallery in Vienna. In 1627, Rubens was employed in diplomatic service at the Hague, and in the next year he was ambassador to Philip IV. of Spain from the Infanta Isabella, widow of the Archduke Albert. In 1629, we find the painter still acting as a diplomatist, and this time to the Court of England. The courtly manner, handsome person, and versatile genius of Rubens made him a favourite at Whitehall. The object of his mission was to arrange a treaty of peace with Spain, and he has been blamed for acting on behalf of the government which so cruelly oppressed his native land. Charles I. of England showed Rubens every mark of favour; he conferred on him the honour of knighthood, and gave him his own sword, and a gold chain which the painter wore ever afterwards. At this period Rubens painted, among many other works, his allegory of *Peace and War*, now in the National Gallery. He also made designs for the great ceiling-piece for Whitehall, a work completed in his Antwerp studio.

On his return to Antwerp, in 1630, he married his second wife, Helena Fourment, a girl of sixteen, belonging to one of the richest families in the city. She served him many times as a model for his pictures. In the collection of pictures at Blenheim are two portraits of the fair Helena; one picture represents Rubens and his wife in a flower garden with a child in leading strings, a work described by Dr. Waagen as one of the most perfect family pictures in the world (Fig. 42). The great master died in 1640, wealthy, honoured, and famous, not only in his own city, but in many another. He was buried in the Church of St. Jacques at Antwerp.

GFDP

✗ Rubens was an almost universal genius in his art, and has left a vast number of pictures dealing with nearly every kind of subject. He painted pictures sacred and secular, studies of animals, portraits of men and women, grand historical and mythological works, and charming landscapes. The great number of works attributed to him would seem almost fabulous, if we did not believe that many of them were really executed under the eye of the master by the pupils who worked from his designs.

We shall only attempt to indicate a few of the most celebrated works of Rubens. As we have said already, what we miss most in his pictures is *soul*. There is a healthy animalism pervading his works, which however much in keeping with the picture of a grand old lion, or a naked, coarse-limbed Flemish woman, is out of place in tragic or domestic scenes,—scenes which Rubens delighted to paint. The heart of the painter does not seem to have beaten one whit faster, nor his hand to have trembled with the slightest emotion, when he undertook the most sublime and most stirring of subjects. The mechanical work is executed to perfection, but it is like Pygmalion's statue, beautiful but soulless. Sir Joshua Reynolds says of Rubens, " He is the best workman with his tools that ever managed a pencil ; " and Coleridge remarks of him, that " So long as he confines himself to space, and outward figure—to the mere animal man with animal passions—he is, I may say, a god among painters. His Satyrs, Silenuses, lions, tigers, and dogs are godlike ; but the moment he attempts anything involving or presuming the spiritual, his gods or goddesses, his nymphs and heroes, become beasts, absolute unmitigated beasts."

It is interesting to notice the contrast afforded by Rubens to the masters of the Dutch School with whom he was cotemporary. Although having some superficial resemblance, the sources from which the Flemish master drew his subjects, and the aims which he had in view, are totally different from those of the Dutchmen.

FIG 42,—RUBENS AND HELENA FOURMENT. BY RUBENS.
At Blenheim.

II 2

Rubens, living in the Spanish Netherlands, where the Roman
Catholic faith remained the religion of the country, represents
in his pictures the historic school of the old faith; whilst the
art of Holland, springing into life with the birth of national
freedom, depicts scenes of every-day life; and their religion, when
there is any, is the religion of the Reformation.

In speaking briefly of the chief works of Rubens, we come
first to the *Descent from the Cross,* in Antwerp Cathedral (Fig. 43).
We find in this wonderful work perfect unity, and a nobler conception and more finished execution than usual. Of the colouring it is needless to speak. But even here in this masterpiece
we notice the absence of spirituality. The dead Christ is an
unidealized study, magnificently painted and drawn, but unre-
deemed by any divinity of form, or pathos of expression in the
head, so that we discover no foregleam of the resurrection:
it is a dead body, no more. This picture was painted originally
for the company of Archers at Antwerp, upon whose land Rubens
had encroached in building his magnificent house. The Archers
requested a picture of St. Christopher in compensation, and the
painter liberally gave more than was asked, and painted all who
had ever earned the name of Christ-bearer. The Archers not
understanding this treatment of the subject, Rubens added a
picture of *St. Christopher* on one of the wings of the vast triptych,
of which the *Descent from the Cross* forms the central panel.
Another picture in the cathedral, almost equally famous, the
Raising of the Cross, afforded him an opportunity for the display
of his extraordinary powers of drawing and painting in the rendering of vigorous action, which in this picture hardly fall short of
Tintoretto. Among the eighteen pictures by Rubens in the Antwerp Museum, is a *Last Communion of St. Francis,* which has a
great reputation, but suffers from the ignoble type of St. Francis's
head. It was painted in 1619. At the Church of St. Jacques
is a so-called *Holy Family,* containing wonderful portraits of
the painter and his own family. St. George is a portrait of

FIG. 43.—DESCENT FROM THE CROSS, BY RUBENS.
In the Cathedral of Antwerp

Rubens, St. Jerome his father, an angel his youngest son; Martha and Mary are respectively Isabella and Helena, the dead and the living wife of Rubens.

In the Gallery at Munich we find ninety-five paintings by this master, illustrating all his styles. The masterpiece is the *Last Judgment.* Of mythological subjects we must notice the *Battle of the Amazons*, and *Castor and Pollux carrying off the Daughters of Leucippus. Seven children carrying a festoon of fruit and flowers* illustrates one of the pleasantest sides of Rubens's art—the painting of children : and several landscapes show us the remarkable power of this universal genius.

Passing to Vienna, we find in the Lichtenstein Gallery the portraits of Rubens's *Two Sons*, and a long series of pictures illustrating the *History of Decius.* In the Belvedere is a magnificent portrait of his second wife, *Helena Fourment ;* also the *Festival of Venus in the Isle of Cythera.* An *Assumption* has two pendents to the right and left, representing *St. Ignatius Loyola curing a Demoniac*, and *St. Francis Xavier preaching to the Indians.* The *Appearance of the Virgin to St. Ildefonso* (Fig. 44) is a vast triptych in which Rubens has shown a union of nobleness, truth, and brilliancy never surpassed by him in any other work.

In the Louvre we find forty-two paintings by Rubens. The greater number of these belong to the series illustrating *The Life of Marie de Medicis.* The *Flight of Lot* is one of the few pictures signed by Rubens, so that he doubtless valued it highly.

At Madrid in the Museo del Rey is a *Glorified Virgin*, a truly wonderful work. Turning to Russia, we find in the Hermitage at St. Petersburg some fine works by this master ; especially deserving of notice is the *Feast in the House of Simon.*

Coming home to England we find this great master again largely represented. The *History of Ixion on the Cloud* is in the gallery of the Duke of Westminster ; and *Diana and her Nymphs surprised by Satyrs,* painted for Charles I. in 1629.

Blenheim contains many great works by Rubens. The *Rape of*

FIG. 44.—THE VISION OF ST. ILDEFONSO. BY RUBENS.
(*The centre-picture of a triptych.*)
In the Belvedere, Vienna.

Proserpine, a *Portrait of Helena Fourment*, and *Portraits of himself, wife and child* (Fig. 42). In the National Gallery among the best specimens are *Peace and War*, the *Rape of the Sabine Women*, the *Horrors of War*, the fine landscape called *Rubens's Château*, and the specially beautiful *Chapeau de Poil* (miscalled the *Chapeau de Paille*).

Before we speak of the pupils of Rubens, we must notice some painters who were his cotemporaries, and worked independently of the great master.

MARTIN PEPYN (1575—1642), a native of Antwerp, occupies a position mid-way between the first decline of Flemish art and its revival under Rubens. There are a few of his pictures in the Antwerp Gallery. A *Portrait of a Lady*, in the Aremburg Gallery at Brussels, is a good specimen of his work.

ABRAHAM JANSSENS, VAN NUYSSEN * (1567—1632), a native of Antwerp, was the scholar of an unimportant master named Snellinck. There is a legend, now disproved, that Janssens was an enemy of Rubens, and fell into great misery. As a fact he lived and died in prosperity. He was sometimes a better draughtsman than Rubens, though far inferior to him in other respects. Many of his pictures have been erroneously attributed to the great Antwerp master. His greatest success was made in representing torch-light scenes, and contrasting bright lights with dark shadows. He is well represented in the galleries of Antwerp and Vienna, and in many of the churches of Flanders.

NICOLAS DE LIEMAKERE, called ROOSE (1575—1646), was born, lived and died in Ghent. His Biblical pictures lack spirituality. One of his chief works is a *Virgin Glorified, adored by Saints*, an altar-piece in one of the chapels of the Cathedral at Ghent.

---

* Janssens frequently added " van Nuijssen " to his name, in order to distinguish himself from another family of the same name. It is thought that it was either the name of his mother or that of the village from which his family came.

Fig. 45.—The Chateau de Steen. By Rubens.

FRANS SNYDERS was celebrated as an animal painter, and ranks second to Rubens. He was born at Antwerp in 1579, and was apprenticed to " Hell " Brueghel, and possibly studied also under Van Balen. He entered the Guild of St. Luke in 1592, was free of it 1602 ; married in 1611 ; became a member of the "Romanists" in 1619, and dean of that society in 1628 ; and died in 1657, and was buried in the church of the Récollets, Antwerp, by the side of his wife, who had been laid there ten years before. As an intimate friend of Rubens, Jordaens, and Van Dyck, Snyders frequently painted animals as well as flowers, fruit, and vegetables for the pictures of his brethren. Doubtless the works of Rubens inspired Snyders, but he was in no sense his pupil. The special power of this master lies in his delineation of wild animals in a state of rage and excitement. He loved to paint a grisly boar rending the hounds with his tusks, or a hunted stag wild with fear and exhaustion. Strongly contrasting with these subjects are the pictures of fruit and flowers, or dead game, in which Snyders also excelled. In England his works are to be found only in private collections. Four large pictures,* two of fish, one of fruit, and one of dead game (Fig. 46), are in the possession of the Duke of Newcastle, at Clumber. In the Louvre we find a *Stag-hunt,* and a *Boar-hunt.* At Dresden is a *Kitchen Scene,* in which the figures are by Rubens. At Munich there are *Two Lionesses pursuing a Roebuck.* His pictures are also to be seen at Berlin and Vienna.

KASPER DE CRAYER † was born at Antwerp in 1582, and was one of the greatest of the cotemporaries of Rubens. He studied at Brussels under Raphael van Coxcien, and was made court-painter by Cardinal Ferdinand, Governor of the Nether-lands. Growing weary of this position, De Crayer retired to Ghent, and there painted some of his most important works,

* Shown at the tenth Exhibition of the works by the Old Masters at Burlington House.

† Frequently written Craeyer.

FIG. 46.—THE POULTERER. BY SNYDERS

among them the *Centurion before Christ*, executed for the Abbey
of Affleghem. It is said that Rubens on seeing this work said :
" Crayer, Crayer, no one will ever surpass you ! " De Crayer
died at Ghent in 1669. Sacred subjects were most congenial to
De Crayer, but he also painted pictures in the departments of allegory and history, but without the grasp of thought, the grandeur,
or the fire of Rubens. In the Ghent Museum he is represented
by the *Coronation of St. Rosalia*, and the *Martyrdom of St.
Blaise*. In the Vienna Gallery we find a *Madonna and Child
adored by Saints*, and there are many of De Crayer's pictures in
Spain.

LUCAS VAN UDEN, a native of Antwerp (1595—1672-73),
was another painter who worked in friendly partnership with
Rubens. He painted some very pleasing landscapes as backgrounds for the great master's works. Both Rubens and David
Teniers returned his kindness by painting figures in the pictures
of Van Uden. His works may be studied in the Dresden Gallery,
which contains seven specimens. In the British Museum are
examples of Van Uden's art as an engraver. He delighted to
paint landscapes with a waterfall, and hills in the distance.

JOOST SUTTERMANS * claims a place among Flemish painters
only from having been born in Antwerp—in 1597. He went
early in life to Florence, and lived and died there, finding
powerful patrons in the Grand Duke Cosmo II. of Tuscany and
his two successors. He died in Florence in 1681. Suttermans
painted historical pictures and portraits, and was as a portrait
painter little inferior to his friend, Van Dyck. In the Uffizi
at Florence is a notable picture from his hand, *The Florentine
Nobility swearing allegiance to Duke Ferdinand II.* " He was
of decided realistic tendency, an able draughtsman, a powerful
and clean colourist, and possessed much freedom of brush. In
his historical pictures the influences both of the schools of the
Carracci and of Michael Angelo Caravaggio are strongly seen.

* Usually written Sustermans.

From the first-named he imitated the style of composition, drapery, and elevated forms; from the latter his commoner truth and powerful effects " (Kugler's ' Handbook ').

THEODOOR ROMBOUTS (1597—1637), after executing several works in Italy, returned to Antwerp, and having been, in 1625, admitted a master of the guild of painters remained there till his death. His chief work is a *Deposition from the Cross*, in Ghent Cathedral.

THE PUPILS OF RUBENS.

ANTOON VAN DIJCK,* the greatest of the pupils of Rubens, the son of a merchant of good standing, was born at Antwerp in 1599. At ten years of age he was studying art under Van Balen, and was registered in the Guild as his pupil; from him he proceeded to the studio of Rubens. His wonderful precocity enabled Van Dyck to become a master in the Guild of Antwerp painters when only nineteen. In 1620 he was engaged as an assistant by Rubens, and in the following year he was in England employed by James I. This royal service soon ended, and in 1623 Van Dyck went to Italy ; in Venice he copied many of Titian's works, and spent some time in Rome, and a much longer time at Genoa. Wherever he went he was busy with brush and canvas, and in Genoa he painted many of his best pictures. From 1626 to 1632 Van Dyck was in Antwerp, diligently working at some of his greatest pictures, historical subjects and portraits. In the Cassel Gallery there are fourteen of his portraits, among which that of the *Syndic Meerstraten* (Fig. 47) is one of the most characteristic of his art at this period. At the close of these six years of Antwerp work a new world opened to him. His first visit to England seems to have been unfruitful, but in 1632 he became one of the court painters of Charles I. Success and honour now

* Or Van Dyck : commonly written Vandyck, and incorrectly, Vandyke.

crowned the new works of Van Dyck. He received a salary of
£200 a year as principal painter to the Stuart court, and was
knighted by the king. Nothing succeeds like success, and we
find Van Dyck sought after by the nobility and gentry of England, and at once installed as a fashionable portrait painter.

He has been called the " Velazquez of Flanders," and indeed the
choice of subjects of the two masters are very similar. Van Dyck
did not use his powers in depicting village maidens, or rustics
carousing ; silk and satin, courtly dresses, and long love-locks
adorn his portraits. Still Van Dyck had a soul above the particular forms of art by which he made money and fame. He
desired to be a great historical artist, and perhaps he might have
been so, had he not become a court painter. He tried in vain to
obtain the task of decorating the Banqueting-Hall in the royal
palace of Whitehall. Later, after his return to Flanders in 1640
with his wife, a lady of the Scottish house of Ruthven, he went
to Paris, hoping to obtain from Louis XIII. the commission to
adorn with paintings the largest saloon in the Louvre, but here
he was doomed to disappointment, as the work had been given
to Poussin. Van Dyck returned to England, and found that he
had fallen, like his patron, Charles I., " on evil tongues and evil
days." The Civil War had commenced. There was no time now
for pipe or tabor, for painting of pictures or curling of love-
locks ; and whilst trumpets were sounding to boot and saddle,
and dark days were coming for England, Van Dyck died in
Blackfriars on the 9th of December in 1641, and was buried hard
by the tomb of John of Gaunt in old St. Paul's.

Possessed of less power of invention than his great master,
Van Dyck shows in his pictures that *feeling* which is wanting
in the works of Rubens. It is infinitely more pleasant to gaze
on a crucifixion, or some other sacred subject, from the pencil of
Van Dyck, than to examine the more brilliant but soulless treatment of similar works by his master. As a portrait painter Van
Dyck occupies with Titian and Velazquez the first place. In fertility

FIG 47.—SYNDIC MEERSTRATEN. BY VAN DYCK.
In the Cassel Gallery.

and production he was equal to Rubens, if we remember that his
artistic life was very brief, and that he died at the age of forty-
two. He lacked the inexhaustible invention which distinguishes
his teacher, and generally confined himself to painting a *Dead
Christ*, or a *Mater Dolorosa*. Of Van Dyck's sacred subjects we
may mention the *Taking of Jesus in Gethsemane* (Museum of
Madrid), *Christ on the Cross* (Munich Gallery), the *Vision of
the Blessed Hermann Joseph* (Vienna), the famous *Madonna with
the Partridges* (St. Petersburg), and a *Dead Christ*, mourned by
the Virgin, and adored by Angels, in the Louvre.

Portraits by Van Dyck are scattered widely throughout the
galleries of Europe, and his best are probably in the private
galleries of England. The melancholy handsome face of the
ill-fated monarch who fought at Naseby and died at Whitehall window is especially associated with the art of Van Dyck.
There is one famous *Portrait of Charles I.* in the Louvre
(Fig. 48), another of the king when twenty-five years old,
in the Hermitage at St. Petersburg. In the Louvre we also
find portraits of *The Three Children of Charles and Henrietta
Maria*, who became subsequently Charles II., James II., and
Mary of Orange. The National Gallery does not contain good
specimens of Van Dyck's work. The so-called *Portrait of
Gevartius* is an exception ; some critics have declared this picture,
which is really the portrait of the art-patron Cornelis van der
Geest, to be the work of Rubens, but Kugler's 'Handbook'
considers it one of the finest from Van Dyck's hand. At Windsor,
among many other of his portraits, is that of the Lady Venetia,
wife of Kenelm Digby, said to have been poisoned by her
husband whilst attempting to heighten her rare beauty by a
potion. Of this picture Hazlitt says, "To perform an unbecoming
action with that portrait hanging in the room would be next to
impossible." In all his portraits there is that air of refinement
and taste which rightly earned for Van Dyck the name which the
Italians gave him, *Pittore Cavalieresco*.

FIG. 48.—KING CHARLES THE FIRST, ATTENDED BY THE MARQUIS OF
HAMILTON. BY VAN DYCK.
In the Louvre.

JACOB JORDAENS, who was born at Antwerp in 1593, worked as a friend in the studio of Rubens. Having married the daughter of his first master Van Noort, Jordaens was obliged to stay at home, and thus escaped the contagion of Italian plagiarism. To this fact we owe the vigorous, though coarse, originality of his style. He possessed much of the fire and impetuosity of Rubens, and equals him in power of colour. "In a certain golden glow and depth of chiaroscuro he even excels him" (Kugler's 'Handbook'). Still Jordaens remains what he has been called, "a vulgar Rubens." His sacred subjects have little or nothing sacred about them except the name; the best specimen is an *Adoration of the Shepherds*, in the Antwerp Museum. In the field of humorous art, however, Jordaens is a master, although his humour is almost utterly devoid of delicacy and taste. Intensely realistic in his pictures, his realism often degenerates into coarseness and vulgarity. His greatest picture in the department of history and allegory is the *Triumphal Entry of the Prince of Nassau*, executed in fresco, in the House in the Wood near the Hague, a picture which Sir Joshua Reynolds characterized as "a confused business." The Museum at Brussels is the best place for the study of Jordaens. In *The Miracle of St. Martin* we find the fiery colour as well as the true force which often marked the master. An allegorical painting representing the *Occupation and Gifts of Autumn* is considered one of his finest works. On the whole, however, Jordaens is most himself when depicting, as was his wont, such scenes as the *Musical Party*, where we have an illustration of the old Netherlandish proverb, "As the old ones sing, so the young ones pipe" (Zo de ouden zongen, zo pypen de jongen). A good example of this subject is in the Berlin Gallery. Jordaens achieved considerable success as a portrait painter. He died at Antwerp in 1678.

THEODOOR VAN TULDEN was born at Bois-le-duc in 1607 (?). He was both painter and engraver, and was apprenticed at

Antwerp, where he subsequently became one of Rubens's favourite pupils, and assisted his master in the picture of the *Apotheosis of Marie de Medicis.* He was free of the Guild of Antwerp in 1625, and ten years later he married Maria, daughter of the painter Hendrik van Balen. He died at Bois-le-duc in 1676 (?). In the Louvre we have an *Appearance of Christ to the Virgin,* and in the Berlin Museum a *Triumph of Galatea,* both good specimens of Van Tulden's later works. We find his pictures in many churches of the Netherlands. The influence of the French School, in which he studied, is to be traced in his latest works.

ERASMUS QUELLIN (1607—1678) was a man of education and refinement, who abandoned the study of philosophy for that of art, under Rubens. He aimed even higher than his master's style, but did not attain his mark. He may be studied in the museum and churches of Antwerp.

JAN VAN DEN HOECKE * (1598—1651) was one of Rubens's best scholars both as an historical and portrait painter. He settled in Antwerp, his native town, as court-painter to the Archduke Leopold Wilhelm, Stadtholder of the Spanish Netherlands. In the Vienna Gallery are two portraits of his patron which favourably illustrate the powers of Van den Hoecke. Of the many other disciples of Rubens, it will suffice merely to mention the names of DEODAAT DEL MONT (1582—1644): CORNELIS SCHUT (1597—1655): FRANS WOUTERS (1612—1659): PIETER VAN MOL (1599—1650): and WILLEM VAN HERP (1604—1677).

We pass on to consider some painters of Flanders who were not pupils of Rubens, although a few of them were imitators.

DAVID TENIERS, the elder, was born at Antwerp in 1582; his father was Julian Teniers; he is said also to have been a pupil of Rubens, but the best critics fail to discover any traces in his works of the great master's influence. Teniers visited

* Miscalled Van Hoeck.

I 2

Rome when quite a youth, and there received his most important lessons in art from Adam Elshaimer. On his return from
Rome, after a lengthened stay, he resided in Antwerp, painting
diligently till his death, in 1649. His favourite subjects were
genre pictures and landscapes. The Dresden Gallery contains
seven pictures of the elder David Teniers : the National Gallery
possesses three. In the church of St. Paul, Antwerp, is a
picture of his called the *Seven Works of Mercy.* His mythologic
and historic pictures are the least successful of his works.

DAVID TENIERS, the younger, was the third great master
of the Netherlands, and the greatest genre painter of his
country. He has been called the "Proteus of painting," and
indeed he ranged through almost every kind of subject, "from
grave to gay, from lively to severe ; " now making us laugh at
his merry peasants keeping revel at a tavern, anon depicting in
terrible colours the horrors of war ; at one time introducing us
to witches and goblins, who are more grotesquely comic than
terrible, at another showing us Biblical scenes which excite any
feeling rather than that of reverence. Teniers declared that it
would need a gallery, two leagues in length, to contain all his
pictures. Born at Antwerp in 1610, he received his earliest lessons
in art from his father. Whether he was a pupil of Rubens is
doubtful, but the influence of that master is traceable in the
pictures of Teniers. In 1632–33 he became free of the
Guild at Antwerp. In 1637 he married Anne, daughter of
Velvet Brueghel. By this marriage he had seven children,
and from a second marriage in 1656, four children. In
1644–45, Teniers was Dean of the Guild of St. Luke, and in
1663 he was instrumental in the erection of the Academy of
Fine Arts, in connection with the Guild. The Archduke Leopold
William, Governor of the Spanish Netherlands, became his
patron, and appointed Teniers to be court painter, groom of the
chamber, and superintendent of his picture gallery—appoint-
ments which were confirmed in 1656 by Don Juan of Austria,

when he succeeded the Archduke as governor. Under such patronage he soon became prosperous and popular, and lived in grand style at his château of "de drij Toren" (Three Towers) at Perck, between Vilvorde and Mechlin, entertaining noblemen and art patrons, who made a point of visiting the painter. Here he died in 1690, and was buried in the church of Perck,

FIG. 49.—THE KNIFE-GRINDER. BY TENIERS.

hard by his home, without stone or epitaph to record his life and labours. A portion of the old château, where among other guests Teniers entertained Don Juan, natural son of Philip IV. of Spain, still remains, but it has degenerated into an inartistic farm-house. Queen Christina of Sweden and Philip IV. of Spain were magnificent patrons of Teniers.

The best works of Teniers belong to his middle, or " silver period," when they are distinguished by a soft silver hue. Bürger* says of him : " The pictures belonging to his middle life are the best. In his youth he followed his father too implicitly ; in his old age his imagination became somewhat stereotyped, and his hand somewhat heavier. Teniers is like one of the fishes which he painted so well, excellent between the head and tail." The vast numbers of pictures executed by Teniers in a working life of more than half a century are scattered widely. At Madrid there are fifty-three, at St. Petersburg forty, at Dresden thirty, at Vienna eighteen, at Munich fourteen, in the Louvre fifteen, in the National Gallery nineteen ; others cannot be traced. To speak at any length of this versatile master's works—of his guard-rooms with old armour, of his landscapes and cattle-pieces, his monkeys and cats feasting, his village revels and tavern - drinking - bouts, and other subjects as widely distant from each other as the poles—would of course be impossible here. We can only indicate a few specimens of his almost universal art. In the Louvre we find many of Teniers's after-dinner pieces, so-called because they were completed between dinner and bed-time. There, too, are the *Temptation of St. Anthony*, full of grotesque humour, and his *Peter denying Christ*, in which work a number of Walloon soldiers are playing cards. Teniers carried the realism of every-day life into all his pictures, and though perfectly at home in a tavern scene, was utterly out of place in a sacred subject. In the Louvre also we find his picture of the *Prodigal Son.* In the various peasant scenes, which he studied from life, Teniers is unsurpassed, and resembles the Dutch School more closely than any of his countrymen. Greuze said of him : " Show me a pipe, and I will tell you if the smoker is by Teniers " (Fig. 50).

At Vienna we find the *Sacrifice of Isaac,* in the Belve-dere ; the *Fête de Sablons*, in the gallery of the Archduke

* The *nom de plume* of M. Thoré.

FIG. 50.—THE PEASANT WITH THE BEER-JUG. BY TENIERS THE YOUNGER.

Leopold; and the *Seven Works of Mercy*, in the Buda-Pesth Gallery (formerly the Esterhazy Collection). At Munich there is the *Italian Fair*, a huge picture measuring three yards by four. At Madrid, the Museo del Rey contains among other pictures by Teniers the famous *Picture Gallery visited by Gentlemen*, describing the work which the master had done for the Archduke Leopold William. At the Hermitage, St. Petersburg, we must notice a *Kitchen*, containing fish, fruit, and game, in which Teniers has painted his father as a blind fisherman, and himself as a falconer; a view of his château of *Drij Toren*, and the *Archers of Antwerp*, a vast work painted in 1643 for the Guild of Archers. In the National Gallery we may mention another picture of *Drij Toren*, the *Four Seasons*, and the *Fête aux Chaudrons*.

Teniers had many pupils and imitators, many of whom not only copied, or tried to copy, his style, but signed his name to their works. His brother ABRAHAM TENIERS (1629—1670–71): JOOS VAN CRAESBEECK (1608?— living in 1654): DAVID RIJCKAERT (1612 — 1662): and FRANS DUCHATEL (1625—1694?), belong to this category.

GONZALO (or as he wrote it himself GONZALES) COQUES,* who was born at Antwerp in 1614, gained the name of the "Little Van Dyck," from his fondness for that master's style, and the success with which he sometimes approached it. He lived at Antwerp, and was apprenticed to Peeter Brueghel, the third of this name. His best pictures are to be found in England, notably his group of *Family Portraits* in the National Gallery, and full-length portraits of *Charles I. and Henrietta Maria*, in the Bridgwater Gallery. Coques died at Antwerp in 1684.

PIETER VAN DER FAES, who was born at Soest in 1618, is better known as Sir PETER LELY, the painter of the fair and frail beauties of the court of Charles II. The story that he gained the name of Lely from the sign of a lily over the

* Or Cocx.

FIG. 51.—PORTRAIT OF THE COUNTESS DE GRAMMONT. BY LELY.
At Hampton Court.

perfumer's shop where he lived is now generally discredited.
His father, a captain of infantry, changed his name Van der
Faes to Lely.   Sir Peter did for the court of the second Charles
what Van Dyck did for that of the first, but his style is more
artificial, and his colouring is inferior.   He painted portraits for
Charles I., and for Cromwell as well as for Charles II., by whom
he was knighted.   His chief pictures are in Hampton Court.
The best is the *Portrait of the Countess de Grammont* (Fig. 51).
He died in London in 1680.

Of animal painters belonging to this period we must mention
PAUWEL DE VOS, a native of Aelst.   He ably followed up the
class of subjects of which Snyders was the greatest master; in
colour and power of touch he was not far behind Snyders, but
was greatly his inferior in drawing and taste.   At Madrid there
are good examples of his pictures.   He died in 1678.

JAN FYT * was born at Antwerp in 1609; studied under Jan
van Berch; was free of the Guild of St. Luke in 1629 : visited
Italy, and studied in Rome : entered in 1650 the Society of
Romanists at Antwerp on his return, and in 1652 became Dean
of the Society, and died in that city in 1661.   Jan Fyt is, after
Snyders, the greatest animal painter of the Flemish School.   He
was specially successful as a painter of greyhounds and hares;
no one has equalled him in this special branch of his art.   The
fur of his animals and the plumage of his birds seem instinct
with life; and his pictures lose no breadth from the extraordinary
minuteness with which he rendered every hair and feather in his
still-life subjects.   We find him well represented at Munich,
Vienna, and Dresden.   At the Dresden Gallery six fine pictures
of *Dead Game*, and in the Antwerp Gallery *Two Dogs sleeping*,
are good specimens of Jan Fyt's work; some of his choicest
works are to be found in the collection of Sir Richard Wallace,
and in numerous other private galleries of England.

ADRIAAN VAN UTRECHT, who was born at Antwerp in 1599, is

* Properly Fijt : written also, but incorrectly, Feyt, Feydt, and even Vyt.

a master whose works abound in most continental galleries. He painted chiefly kitchen scenes, with game and fowls, alive and dead. He travelled in France, Italy, and Germany, and settled in Antwerp, where he died in 1652–53.

JACOB VAN ES (or ESSEN), who was born at Antwerp in 1606, another painter of this class, was specially successful in depicting fish and marine animals. His pictures of *Fish Markets*, in the Vienna Gallery, are good examples. He died at Antwerp in 1665–66.

In the department of landscape painting we find several Flemish artists, who all, more or less, copied the French style of painting, some of them becoming followers of Gaspard Poussin. Hilly landscapes, richly wooded, are the favourite subjects of some of these ; others choose a more ideal class of subjects, like that of Poussin.

JACOBUS VAN ARTOIS * was born in 1613, at Brussels, and died some time after 1684. He was a pupil of Jan Martens, an otherwise unknown painter, but principally studied from nature. His landscapes are found in most of the public galleries abroad, and are also to be met with in the private collections in England.

CORNELIS HUYSMANS (1648—1727), a native of Antwerp, was a pupil of Jacobus van Artois; his pictures are smaller, and his subjects more ideal. The forest of Soignes, near Brussels, was his favourite resort for study. Powerful drawing and brilliant glowing colour distinguish his pictures.

GERARD DE LAIRESSE (1641—1711), a pupil of his father Reinier de Lairesse, and of Bertholet Flemalle, was born at Liege : he has been styled "the Poussin of Belgium." In Utrecht and Amsterdam he was very famous ; but he became totally blind in 1690. Lairesse's works were executed in the classic style, and with great ability. In the Dresden Gallery we find his *Apollo and the Muses on Mount Parnassus ;* other pictures by him are in the Louvre and Berlin Galleries.

* Or Artcys—frequently called Jacques d'Arthois.

JEAN FRANÇOIS MILLET, comonly called FRANCISQUE, was born at Antwerp in 1642, his father being a Frenchman. Millet settled in Paris, and formed his art upon the model of the two Poussins. "He did not attain the beauty of line and purity of drawing which characterized the Poussins, but his compositions are elevated in taste, and his colouring, though betraying a certain monotony, is warmer and clearer than that of his models" (Kugler's 'Handbook'). Millet died in Paris in 1680.

JAN FRANS VAN BLOEMEN (1662—1740), a native of Antwerp, studied chiefly in Rome, and almost exclusively from the works of Gaspard Poussin. From the extreme beauty of the distances of his landscapes he has been called ORIZONTE. Many of his pictures are at Rome, Vienna, Dresden, and Paris.

Flemish art, which had rapidly declined after Teniers, and was almost dead at the close of the seventeenth century, was partly revived by the school of the French painter David. It was not, however, till the beginning of the present century that a true revival took place. The Belgian School, which seems destined to hold an important and lasting position in the world of art, owes its establishment to

JEAN AUGUSTE HENRI LEYS, who was born at Antwerp in 1815. Originally educated for holy orders, he commenced studying art, in the year 1830, with his brother-in-law Ferdinandus de Braekeleer, and in 1833 produced his picture of a *Combat between a Grenadier and a Cossack*, exhibited at Antwerp. Another picture at Brussels, *La Furie Espagnole*, excited much attention, and its author became rapidly famous. Honours crowded thick upon him, and he was made a Baron, and a member of the Legion of Honour. In the London Exhibition of 1862, Baron Leys exhibited, among other pictures, part of a series executed for the town-hall of Antwerp, illustrative of the *Freedom of Belgium*. After his death, in 1869,

FIG. 52.—LUTHER AS CHOIR-BOY IN THE STREETS OF EISENACH. BY LEYS.

his body lay in state, like that of Raphael, with his favourite work, *Margaret and the Magistrates of Antwerp*, above his head. "He was," says a critic, "a man who sought beauty in the human figure and face for its own sake. . . . . A fine, powerful, and variously-endowed colourist—really a colourist in the true sense of the term." His earlier works are evidently inspired by the study of Rembrandt; but later on he changed his style, and adopted the manner of the earlier Flemish School, which gives a certain quaintness to his work; but his pictures are in no sense imitations, for they are always carefully studied from nature, and admirably true. He is one of the few modern painters whose works will stand by the side of the old masters (Fig. 52).

GUSTAVUS WAPPERS, who was born at Antwerp in 1803, received his first instruction in art from Matthias van Bree and Guillaume Jacques Herreynes. Unsuccessful in his endeavours to gain the travelling prize for Italy, he turned his attention towards the works of Rubens and Van Dyck. Then at Paris, he was somewhat influenced by the new movement of the romantic school. On his return to Belgium in 1830 he exhibited *The Self-Devotion of the Burgomasters of Leyden;* a work which gained well-merited praise: and he shortly became the centre of attraction and the head of numerous pupils. It would be impossible here to give a list of his works, which were mostly historical. He received commissions and honours without ceasing — amongst others, the Director-ship of the Academy at Antwerp (which post he resigned in 1853), and the post of painter to the King of the Belgians, with the rank of Baron, and the Presidency of the Belgian National Museum. He died in Paris in 1874.

The noble work of reforming the art of Belgium commenced by Leys is being well carried out by Louis Gallait and others.

PAINTING IN HOLLAND.

FIG. 52A.—EULENSPIEGEL.
From an Engraving by Lucas van Leyden.

BOOK III.

THE DUTCH SCHOOL (1450—1700).

CHAPTER I.

BEFORE speaking of the general characteristics of Dutch art, and of that brilliant School which made Holland of the seventeenth century as famous in painting as in war, we must notice briefly an earlier and little-known Dutch School, totally distinct in character and aims from that of the later masters. This School of the fifteenth century, which was really more Flemish than Dutch in its character, was founded by ALBERT VAN OUWATER, at Haarlem. He lived in the early part of the fifteenth century, and none of his works are now remaining.

GEERTGEN VAN SINT JANS,* or GERARD OF HAARLEM, a pupil of Van Ouwater, differs very little in character and style from the old masters of Cologne, Wilhelm and Stephan. There are two pictures attributed to him in the Vienna Gallery, one the *Legend of the Bones of St. John the Baptist;* the other a *Pietà.* Geert-

---

* So called from a monastery of the Knights of St. John at Haarlem.

GFDP   K gen flourished probably in the sixteenth century. He is said to have died at the early age of twenty-eight.

HIERONYMUS VAN AEKEN, commonly called JEROM BOSCH from his birth-place Hertogenbosch (Bois-le-Duc), was born between 1460 and 1464. He painted pictures in which weird and fantastic subjects abound. That he visited Spain, as has often been asserted, is sometimes doubted : at all events he did not make a long stay there. He died at his birthplace in 1518. The Museum of Madrid contains several of his works.

CORNELIS ENGELBRECHTSEN, who was born at Leyden in 1468, was probably the first artist in that city who painted in oil. In the town-hall of Leyden there is an authentic work from his hand ; the centre picture represents the *Crucifixion*, and at the two sides are the *Sacrifice of Abraham* and the *Lifting of the Brazen Serpent*. Engelbrechtsen, who died in 1533, was the master of a far more important painter of this school—

LUCAS JACOBSZ, better known as LUCAS VAN LEYDEN (1494—1533). During his brief life of thirty-nine years Lucas was the friend of many great artists, among whom were Quinten Matsys, Dürer, and Mabuse. He is said to have been acknowledged as a master before he was twelve years old, and had at that early age became famous as a painter, engraver, and wood-carver. Lucas must have been well off, as he was wont to travel in grand style, and to entertain his brother artists in princely fashion. He is better known from his engravings (Fig. 53) than his oil paintings ; the latter are rare, and difficult of access. In the town-hall at Leyden is a *Last Judgment ;* at the Munich Gallery is a *Crucifixion ;* in the Royal Collection at Buckingham Palace is an important *Adoration of the Magi ;* and at Wilton House the Earl of Pembroke possesses a *Card Party*, from the hand of Lucas van Leyden. He treated sacred subjects with a whimsical and grotesque realism, which is the characteristic of his school. Of his engravings, the *Temptation of St. Anthony* is said to have been executed when Lucas was only fifteen. His *Eulen-*

FIG. 53.—VIRGIL IN THE BASKET. BY LUCAS VAN LEYDEN.

spiegel, a queer quaint production, is prized for its scarcity; there are only four or five impressions in existence (Fig. 52A).

It will not be necessary to trace the line of feeble painters who lived between the time of Lucas Van Leyden and Rembrandt. Some of them, like MARTEN VAN VEEN, called from his birthplace VAN HEEMSKERCK (1498—1574), and CORNELIS CORNELISZ, called CORNELIS VAN HAARLEM (1562—1638), went to Italy and lost their national art in following Raphael and Michelangelo; others, like CORNELIS VAN POELENBURG (1586—1667) introduced the taste and style of the Italians into the simplicity of the Netherlands, whilst GERARD VAN HONTHORST (1590 — 1656), called by the Italians " Gherardo delle Notti," painted nothing, as a rule, but lamplight scenes, and so made for himself a specialty in art.

We proceed to speak of that later Dutch School, which, within a period of less than a century, between the birth of Frans Hals (1584), and that of Jan van Huysum (1682), contained the greatest painters which Holland has ever produced. The birth of Dutch art and of Dutch freedom were cotemporaneous. Holland emerged from the long and cruel thraldom of the oppressor to freedom of action and to freedom of thought. It cast off the religion of its taskmasters, and the same religious revolution which created a political Holland created also Dutch art. The religion of the pictures of this school, when there is any, is that of a bald Protestantism which makes their sacred scenes as unlovely as the religious services where Protestantism has sway. The Bible is interpreted in Dutch art not by the Church, but by the people, and the simplicity of Scripture is exaggerated to triviality. In their choice of subject the Dutch masters stand out in sharp contrast to the painters of Italy. The Italians take us into the seventh Heaven, and show us lovely visions of saints and angels, flooded with a golden radiance from on high; the Dutchmen teach us to find an idyll in a broomstick, or a Paradise in a tavern parlour. To their eyes a

girl peeling onions is a worthier subject than a glorified Madonna;
and if they paint sacred pictures, the Dutch Burgomaster and the
homely *Vrouw* peep out from the thin disguise of a Holy Family.

The Dutch School is the exponent of every-day life; it
has no aspirations after the great and glorious, the mysterious
or the unseen. Nature, as seen in Holland, either out of doors
or in the house, is the one inspiration of its art. We have come
to the domain of naturalism, and have left spiritualism in Italy;
just as we have exchanged the blue skies of the South for the
leaden, cloudy atmosphere of the North. We must not suppose,
however, that the Dutch School in its realistic character presents
nothing but a brutal materialism, and never rises above the
delineation of drunken boors at a village inn. There is a *truthfulness* in the Dutch pictures which commands admiration; a
dead tree by Ruisdael may touch a heart, a bull by Paulus Potter
may speak eloquently, a kitchen by Kalf may contain a poem.
All the painters of this school confined themselves to loving,
understanding, and representing nature, every one adding his
own feelings and tastes,—in fact, adding *himself.* This love of
nature is specially shown in those landscapes and sea-pieces in
which the Dutch School excels. If we visit various parts of
Holland in different kinds of weather, we shall see how each
painter identifies *himself* with the special aspect which he depicts.
A barren, gloomy landscape under a leaden sky, unrelieved by
living creature, its grim monotony only broken by a waterfall or
a dead tree, at once shows us Jacob van Ruisdael, "the melancholy
Jacques" of landscape painters, who finds "tongues in trees,
books in the running brooks, sermons in stones." A bright early
morning, when the sun flashes merrily on white sail and glancing
streams, and the fat cattle are browsing knee-deep in the rich
meadows, reminds us of the lover of light, Aelbert Cuyp. A
warm afternoon, when the shadows of the fruit-trees lie across
the orchard, and an ox, or horse, or some other animal, lies in the
grateful shade, tells us of Paulus Potter, the Raphael of animal

painters, the La Fontaine of artists. An evening landscape, where, amid the grazing cattle, some rustic Meliboeus " sports with Amaryllis in the shade," and presents an idyll such as a Dutch Virgil might have written, recalls Adriaan van de Velde. A still pond, with the moon reflected on its surface, and a few cottages nearly hidden by the dark alder and poplar trees, brings before us the painter of the night, Van der Neer. The sea-shore, with high-sterned Dutch ships sailing over the waves, is the favourite haunt of Willem van de Velde ; a river flowing on towards the horizon, and reflecting a dull grey sky, recalls Van Goyen, and if we look on a frozen canal, crowded with skaters, Isack van Ostade stands confessed.

And this is not true only of landscape and sea-pictures ; the every-day life of Holland is identified in its various phases with different painters of this school. Owing to the changes which time and fashion make, we shall not find in the streets of Antwerp the *Night Watch* of Rembrandt, or the *Banquet* of Van der Helst in the town-hall ; the long satin robes of Ter Borch ; the plumed cavaliers of Wouwerman ; or the drunken peasants of Adriaan van Ostade. But if in passing through a Dutch town, we see a young girl leaning over the old balustrades of a window surrounded with ivy and geraniums, we may still recognize Gerard Dou. In the peaceful interior of a Gothic house, where an old woman is spinning, and which is lighted up by the warm rays of the sun, we see Pieter de Hooch. The canal bordered with trees, in a clean town, ever wearing a holiday appearance, where every stone in the streets may be counted, as well as every tile on the roof and every brick in the walls, reminds us of Van der Heyde ; and the vegetable garden at Amsterdam still testifies to the fidelity of Metsu. We have seen, then, that the origin of the Dutch School is to be traced to that epoch when Holland successfully waged the war of Independence, and threw off the yoke of Spain and of the Inquisition. We have seen that the religion of the school is that of a marked

Protestantism, and that in its choice of subjects, Nature stands first, especially the homelier side of nature in every-day life. We may notice, too, that nearly every master of this school stands by himself, delineating nature in his own special way. One word must be said on the *colouring* of the Dutch masters. We frequently find a brilliance of colour in their pictures which we should scarcely expect under the gloomy skies of Holland. The secret is to be found in the double existence of Holland, European and Oriental. Cold and grey as its own skies may be, it possess-d bright lands amongst colonies in the tropics ; and many a Dutch master, as he saw the ships come home laden with the treasures of the East, dreamed of the sun of Java, whilst he saw only the grey shadows of Holland. We have said that the Dutch School contained all its greatest masters within the space of less than a century. That school sprung into vigorous life, full grown as it were, at once, without preparation, and died as quickly.

MICHIEL JANSZ MIEREVELT was born at Delft in 1567, and studied art under Bloklandt at Utrecht. He first painted altar-pieces for the churches of Delft; but, some portraits which he had executed being much admired, he turned his attention towards that branch of art, and subsequently became very successful (Fig. 54). He died at his native Delft in 1641. Mierevelt was a prolific painter. Good specimens of his art are in the town-hall of his native city.

JAN VAN RAVESTEYN, who was born at the Hague, probably in 1572,* was a portrait-painter of no small merit. His chief works are in the town-hall of his native city—the *Civic Guard leaving the 'Doelen'* (1616) ; a *Banquet of the Town Council* (1618) ; a *Meeting of the Town Council* (1636) ; and the *Officers of the Civic Guard* (1638).

As the artists of Italy were employed by princes and prelates to paint, for their chapels, altar-pieces and wall-decorations, into which they had to introduce the portraits of their patrons, either

* Several authorities give 15 0.

as mere spectators or sometimes as participators in the sacred
scene, so in the Burgher-governed Holland of the seventeenth
century such painters as Ravesteyn, Van der Helst, Hals, and
even Rembrandt, were commissioned to execute large corporation
pictures, which partook more of the character of a mass of
portraits crowded into one frame than of an animated scene.
But Rembrandt and Hals emancipated themselves from this
formality, gave composition to their works, individuality to their
sitters, and thus produced *pictures*, and not mere portrait-groups.
To be just to the latter class, however, it must be remembered
that the composition of twenty or thirty figures was not rendered
easier by the fact that each worthy member of the Civic Guard
or Town Council wanted as much of his person to appear as
possible; and the painter, very often, perhaps, had little to do
with the grouping of his picture. They were not all Rembrandts,
to dare to brook the anger of the burghers by arranging their
works as their eye would have them.

Other portraits by Ravesteyn are in the galleries of Berlin,
Munich, Amsterdam, and Brunswick. He died at the Hague
in 1657.

FRANS HALS was born at Antwerp in 1584, and studied
under Karel van Mander at Haarlem, where the rest of his life
was spent. Though the records of his private life are not
pleasant; though he was to some extent a drunkard; ill-
treated his first wife, Anneke Harmansz; and wronged his
second, Lysbeth Reyniers; though he was frequently sued for
debt, was supported in later life by public charity, and died in
poverty—yet he was not the sot that some of his biographers
represented him. There are shadows in his life; but they need
not have been painted in colours black as ink. Moreover, Hals
held posts of honour in Haarlem—scarcely compatible with
continual drunkenness. He was a member of the Guild of
Rhetoric (de Wijngaardranken); of the Civic Guard; and of the
Guild of St. Luke.

FIG. 51.—PORTRAIT OF WILLIAM THE SILENT. BY MIEREVELT.

Hals stands pre-eminent among the portrait-painters of the Dutch-School. He excited the admiration of his contemporary, Van Dyck, whose portrait he is said to have painted with great rapidity when summoned from the ale-house to execute the task. His most notable works are the *Portrait of Himself and his wife Lysbeth* (Amsterdam Museum), the *Banquet of the Officers of the Civic Guard* (Fig. 55), (Haarlem Museum), the *Regents and Regentes* of the hospital where he died (Haarlem Museum), a *Portrait of Hille Bobbe*, the Haarlem fishwife (Berlin Museum); three portraits in the Dresden Gallery ; and one *Portrait of a Woman* in the National Gallery.

Numerous good portraits by Hals are to be found in private collections in England, but it is only of late years that his merits have been appreciated.

The crown and glory of the Dutch School, however, is—

REMBRANDT HARMENSZ,* VAN RIJN. Few persons have suffered more from their biographers than the painters of the Dutch school, and none of them more than Rembrandt. The writings of Van Mander, and the too active imagination of Houbraken, have misrepresented these artists in every possible way. Thus Rembrandt has been described as the son of a miller, one whose first ideas of light and shadow were gained among his father's flour-sacks in the old mill at the Rhine. He has been described as a spendthrift reveller at taverns, and as marrying a peasant girl. All this is fiction. The facts are briefly these: Rembrandt was born on July 15th, 1607, in the house of his father, Hermann Gerritszoon van Rijn, a substantial burgess, the owner of several houses, and possessing a large share in a mill on the Weddesteeg at Leyden. Educated at the Latin school at Leyden, and intended for the study of the law, Rembrandt's early skill as an artist determined his father to allow him to follow his own taste. He studied for a short time under Jacob

* Or Harmenszoon—*i.e.* Rembrandt, the son of Harmen of the Rhine (who was Gerritszoon, *i.e.* the son of Gerrit).

FIG. 55.—BANQUET OF THE OFFICERS OF THE CIVIC GUARD. BY HALS.
In the Haarlem Museum.

van Swanenburch at Leyden, then under Pieter Lastman at Amsterdam, and perhaps also under Jan Pynas at Haarlem.

But it was not from these nor from any master that Rembrandt learnt to paint. Nature was his model, and he was his own teacher. In 1630 he produced one of his earliest oil paintings, the *Portrait of an Old Man* (Cassel Gallery), and at this time he settled as a painter in Amsterdam. He devoted himself to the teaching of his pupils more than to the cultivation of the wealthy, but instead of being the associate of drunken boors, as some have described him, he was the friend of the Burgomaster Six, of Jeremias de Decker the poet, and many other persons of good position. In 1632 Rembrandt produced his famous picture, *The Lesson in Anatomy;* about that time he was established in Sint Antonie Breedstraat; in the next year he married Saskia van Ulenburch, the daughter of the Burgomaster of Leeuwarden, whose face he loved to paint best after that of his old mother. We may see Saskia's portrait in the famous picture, *Rembrandt with his wife on his knee,* in the Dresden Gallery; and a *Portrait of Saskia* alone is in the Cassel Gallery (Fig. 56).

In the year 1640 Rembrandt painted a portrait, long known under the misnomer of *The Frame-maker.** It is usually called 'Le Doreur,' and it is said that the artist painted the portrait in payment for some picture-frames; but is in reality a portrait of Dorer, a friend of Rembrandt. The year 1642 saw Rembrandt's master-piece, the so-called *Night-watch.* Saskia died in the same year, and the four children of the marriage all died early, Titus, the younger son, who promised to follow in his father's steps, not surviving him. Rembrandt was twice married after Saskia's death, first to Hendrickie Jaghers, then to Catharina van Wyck. The latter years of the great master's life were clouded by misfortune. Probably owing to the stagnation of trade in Amsterdam, Rembrandt grew poorer and poorer, and in

* In 1865 it fetched no less than 155,000 francs, at a sale.

FIG. 56.—SASKIA VAN ULENBURCH. BY REMBRANDT.
In the Cassel Gallery

1656 was insolvent. His goods and many pictures were sold by auction in 1658, and realized less than 5000 guilders. Still he worked bravely on. His last known pictures are dated 1668. On the 8th of October in 1669 Rembrandt died, and was buried in the Wester Kerk.

Rembrandt was the typical painter of the Dutch School; his treatment is distinctly Protestant and naturalistic. Yet he was an idealist in his way, and as " the King of Shadows," as he has been called, he brought forth from the dark recesses of nature, effects which become, under his pencil, poems upon canvas. Rembrandt loved to paint pictures warmed by a clear, though limited light, which dawns through masses of shadow, and this gives much of that air of mystery so notice-able in his works. In most of his pictures painted before 1633 there is more daylight and less shadow, and the work is more studied and delicate. To this class of works belongs the *Lesson in Anatomy* (Museum of the Hague), which represents Professor Tulp dissecting a dead body in the presence of several other doctors. The subject exactly suited the realistic character of the painter. M. Maxime du Camp says of this work : " This is a European picture of world-wide renown, which will remain in traditions even after it is destroyed, for it is one of those few things done by men which is perfectly beautiful." In the Museum of Amsterdam, the city where Rembrandt died, is his greatest work, the *Night-watch* (Fig. 57). It is difficult to under-stand why this name has been given to a picture which represents a daylight scene. Its more correct name is the *Sortie of the Com-pany of Frans Banning Cock*. It contains twenty-three figures of life size. They are a band of the civic guard starting to patrol the streets of Amsterdam, and possibly about to shoot at a mark, the prize being a cock which a gaily-dressed girl holds in her hand. The popular name for this picture probably arose from its luminous and transparent tints, the great effects of light and shade, which seem produced by an artificial light rather than

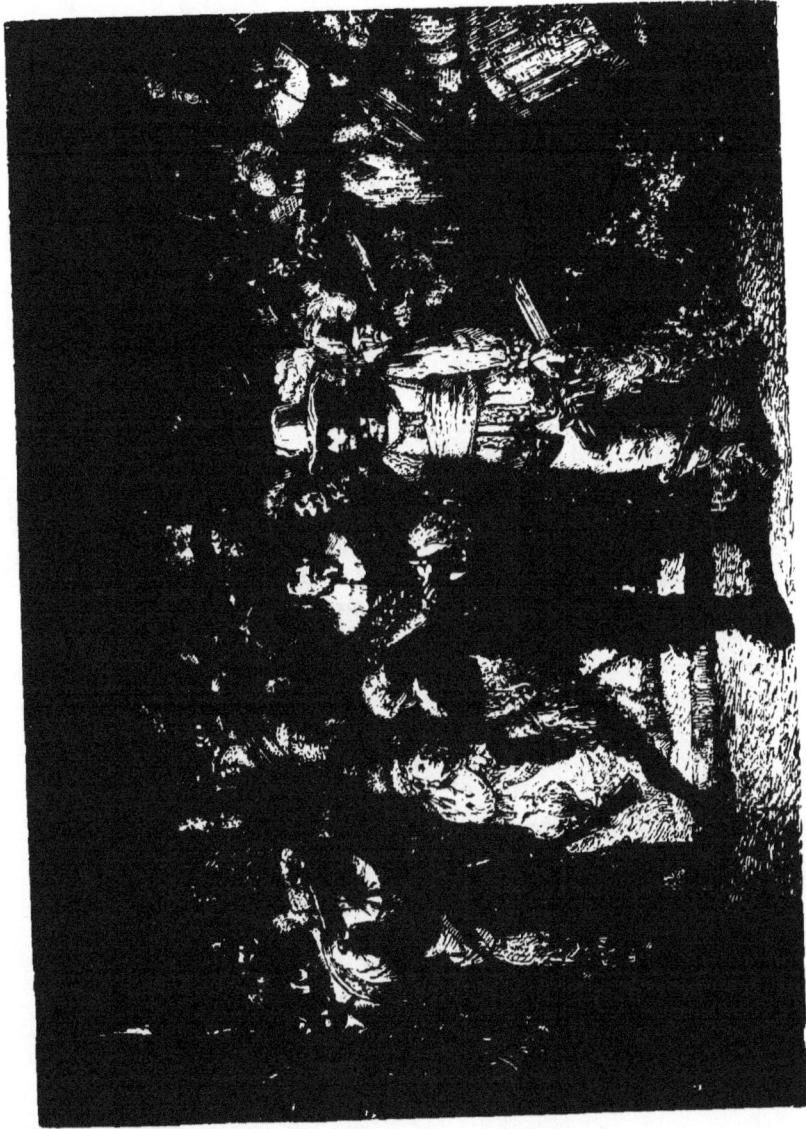

FIG. 57.—THE NIGHT-WATCH. BY REMBRANDT.
In the Museum of Amsterdam.

by the sun. "It is neither the light of the sun, nor of the moon, nor does it come from torches, it is rather the light from the genius of Rembrandt." "The faces of the civic guard represent the popular heroes who saved Holland from Spain. This picture will preserve the remembrance of Dutch liberty, perhaps even beyond the existence of Holland." Another picture by Rembrandt is by some critics placed in a higher rank than the *Night-watch.* This is the collection of portraits of the *Syndics of the Cloth Hall (Staalhof)*, of the year 1661, in the Amsterdam Gallery. We do not, in looking at this picture, seem to see six portraits, but six living men. In the Louvre we may study some very small but exquisite pictures by this master. The *Philosophers in Meditation*, and the *House of an old Carpenter*, (probably intended for a *Holy Family*), show to perfection that poetry of naturalism of which Rembrandt was the great teacher. In the National Gallery we find two portraits of Rembrandt, one representing him at the age of thirty-two, another when an old man. In the same collection is the *Woman taken in Adultery* (1644), and the *Adoration of the Shepherds* (1646), both superb in arrangement and execution. Germany and Russia are almost as rich as Holland in the number of Rembrandt's pictures which they possess. The *Descent from the Cross*, in the Munich Gallery, is a specimen of the sacred subjects of this master. He interprets the Bible from the Protestant and realistic standpoint, and though the colouring of the pictures is marvellous, the grotesque features and Walloon dress of the personages represented make it hard to recognize the actors in the gospel story. Many of his Scripture characters were doubtless painted from the models afforded him in the Jews' quarter of Amsterdam where he resided. Every one knows the portraits painted and etched by Rembrandt; he delighted to draw the heads of old people, in which every wrinkle and line are faithfully delineated, and every emotion of the sitter is expressed. In his landscapes Rembrandt again shows his profound feeling for the poetry of

FIG. 58.—ECCE HOMO.
From an etching by Rembrandt.

GFDP   L

nature, and invests the cold, cheerless scenery of Holland with beauty. The magnificent panoramic landscape belonging to Lord Overstone, and the famous picture of *The Mill* against a sunset sky, are signal examples of his poetic power, and his etchings show us this peculiarity of his genius even more than his oil paintings. Of these etchings, which range over every class of subject, religious, historical, landscape, and portrait, there is a fine collection in the British Museum; and they should be studied in order to understand the immense range of his superb genius. The *Ecce Homo* (Fig. 58), to say nothing of the splendour, the light and shade, and richness of execution, has never been surpassed for dramatic expression; and we forgive the commonness of form and type in the expression of touching pathos in the figure of the Saviour; nor would it be possible to express with greater intensity the terrible raging of the crowd, the ignobly servile and cruel supplications of the priests, or the anxious desire to please on the part of Pilate. The celebrated plate *Christ healing the Sick* exhibits in the highest perfection his mastery of chiaroscuro, and the marvellous delicacies of gradation which he introduced into his more finished work. The number of Rembrandt's pictures in Holland, although it includes his three greatest, is remarkably small—indeed they may be counted on the fingers; and lately, by the sale of the Van Loon collection, the Dutch have lost two more of his finest works in the portraits of the *Burgomaster Six* and *His Wife*. But his works abound in the other great galleries of Europe.

Of the pupils of Rembrandt many attained to great excellence as portrait-painters; in other works they are frequently but the shadow of the great master. The first pupil who was received by Rembrandt was GERARD DOU, but it will be more convenient to speak of him later among other Dutch genre-painters.

Among the students and imitators whom the great master kept penned up at work at the top of his house, each partitioned off from his neighbour, was—

Fig. 59.—Portrait of Bol. By himself

FERDINAND BOL who in his early days followed closely the style of Rembrandt. Of his life little is known. He was born at Dordrecht in 1611; was taken when still a child by his parents to Amsterdam, of which he was made a citizen. There he resided until his death in 1681. A woman's portrait in the Berlin Museum, date 1642, shows this earlier and better form of Bol's art. Later in life he forsook his great teacher's manner entirely, and his historical pictures show indifferent workmanship, and his colouring displays less refinement. Bol excelled as a portrait-painter (Fig. 59). His master-piece is *The Four Regents of the Lepers' Hospital*, in the town-hall, Amsterdam. In the National Gallery we have a *Portrait of an Astronomer* from his hand. He is also well represented at Dresden and St. Petersburg.

JACOB BACKER * was born at Harlingen in 1608 (or 1609). He first studied under Lambert Jacobsz at Leeuwarden, and then with Rembrandt, whose studio he entered between 1632 and 1634. He resided chiefly at Amsterdam, where he died in 1651. Backer, like Bol, adhered to the style of Rembrandt in his earlier works, as we may see by studying his portraits of himself and his wife in the Museum at Brunswick. The picture of *The Syndics*, in the Van der Hoop collection at Amsterdam, illustrates the later period when he had sought other sources of inspiration. Backer was celebrated for the extreme facility and rapidity of his work. It was his wont, it is said, to finish a portrait in a day. He was also successful as an historical painter.

GOVAERT FLINCK was born at Cleves in 1615. Like Backer, he first studied under Lambert Jacobsz at Leeuwarden, and then with Rembrandt at Amsterdam, where he took the freedom in 1652, and resided until his death in 1660. Flinck was the friend as well as the pupil of Rembrandt. He painted his master's portrait, and Rembrandt, in return, painted those of

* Or Bakker, not to be confounded with Jacob de Backer of Antwerp,

Flinck and his wife. Next to Van den Eckhout he approaches Rembrandt most closely; and many of his pictures have been mistaken for those of the great master. In his latter years he imitated Murillo with considerable success. He was also distinguished as a painter of genre subjects, but especially in portraiture. Of his historical paintings, *Isaac blessing Jacob* is the best. Among his portraits we may specially notice those in the *Banquet of the Civic Guard*: both these pictures are in the Amsterdam Museum.

PHILIPS DE KONINCK (or KONING), who was born at Amsterdam in 1619, studied under Rembrandt, and became a very good painter of landscapes, into which figures were introduced by Lingelbach and Dirk van Bergen. He sometimes painted portraits, and *occasionally*, it is said, executed historical pieces. He is represented in the galleries of Amsterdam and the Hague. A *Landscape, a View in Holland*, in the National Gallery, is a very good example of his style; in the same collection there is a Hilly Woody Landscape, also by him. De Koninck died at Amsterdam in 1689.

GERBRAND VAN DEN ECKHOUT was born in 1621 at Amsterdam, there studied under Rembrandt and painted, and died there in 1674. He imitated very successfully Rembrandt's style, especially in his treatment of Biblical subjects. In power and in colour he sometimes came very near to his master. He painted many portraits, and also genre subjects. His works may be seen in most public galleries. We may specify *Ruth and Boaz* (Rotterdam Museum), and the *Raising of Jairus's Daughter* (Berlin Museum).

JAN VICTORS is an artist the dates of whose birth and death are unknown. He has been often confounded with Victor Wolfvoet of Antwerp, and Jacob Victor, the painter of poultry. He sometimes signed his name Victor, Victoor, or Fictoor. He probably worked in Rembrandt's studio from about 1635 to 1640. The dates on his works extend from 1640 to 1662. In his Biblical subjects Victor imitates Rembrandt. more closely than in his other works. Of his Old Testament pieces we may mention, *Joseph explaining his Dream*, dated 1648 (Amsterdam Gallery), and *Tobias giving thanks for the recovery of his sight* (Munich Gallery). An *Isaac blessing Jacob*, in the Dulwich Gallery, formerly ascribed to Rembrandt, is given by Dr. Richter to Victors. Of other subjects we have *The Pork Butcher*, and *The Dentist* (Van der Hoop collection, Amsterdam), and a *Village Wedding* (Antwerp Gallery).

JAN DE BRAY, a native of Haarlem, was a very fair portrait. and historical painter of his time. In the town-hall of Haarlem. are some of his best corporation pieces, two of them are *Lady Regents of the Hospital ;* and in the Amsterdam Gallery he is represented by the *Syndics of the Guild of St. Luke of Haarlem,* dated 1675. It contains seven figures in all, of which four are by Jan de Bray ; one, a portrait of Jan himself, is by his brother Dirk, who also figures in the picture. The remaining two are autographic portraits of Jan van Goting and Jan de Jong. Jan de Bray died in 1697.

KAREL FABRITIUS, or FABER, who was born about 1624, was a pupil of Rembrandt ; he might have become famous had he not met with a premature death by the explosion of a powder magazine at Delft in 1654. A fine *Head of a Man* (Rotterdam Museum) by Fabritius, was for a long time ascribed to Rembrandt. Fabritius was the instructor of Jan ver Meer, of Delft.

SAMUEL VAN HOOGSTRAETEN was born at the Hague probably in 1627. He studied under his father Dirk van Hoogstraeten a native of Antwerp, and with Rembrandt. After visiting Vienna, Rome, and London, he settled in his native country, and worked at the Hague and at Dordrecht, where he died in 1678. Van Hoogstraeten painted portraits, landscapes, and still. life. Best among his genre pictures is that of a *Sick Girl,* dressed in light colours (Van der Hoop collection).

NICOLAAS MAES (or MAAS) was born at Dordrecht in 1632. But little is known of his life. He studied under Rembrandt at Amsterdam; and then went about 1660–65 to Antwerp, but

FIG. 60.—THE IDLE SERVANT.
By Nicolaas Maes.

returned to Amsterdam in 1678, and died there in 1693. Maes followed Rembrandt closely in his earlier works. After painting grave subjects for some time, he devoted himself to portraits with great success.   His *Old Woman Spinning,* and a *Girl at a Window,* are in the Amsterdam Gallery.   The *Portrait of a Child of the Burgomaster Six,* and the *Eavesdropper,* are in the Six Gallery.   In England we have in the National Gallery, *The Cradle, The Dutch Housewife,* and *The Idle Servant* (similar in composition to Fig. 60) ; the two last signed and dated, " N. Mæs, 1655."   His genre subjects are less trivial than those of many of his brethren ; and often present beautiful little idylls of Dutch home life.

FIG. 61.—FROM AN ETCHING BY REMBRANDT.

CHAPTER II.

DUTCH PAINTERS OF DOMESTIC LIFE.

WE pass on from the immediate pupils of Rembrandt to notice those artists who, though independent of him, were all more or less influenced by the great founder of the Dutch School. It will be more convenient to consider these painters under four classes: (1) Painters of domestic life, interiors, and portraits. (2) Painters of landscapes and battles. (3) Painters of sea-pieces. (4) Painters of still life, game, architecture, etc.

The Dutch genre painters generally preferred an interior to an out-door scene for their subjects; the character of their climate explains the reason. The Italian, dwelling in a soft, sunny climate, loved to paint out-of-door life, and to depict the blue skies beneath which life was a long holiday. A Dutchman's idea of happiness, on the contrary, was a snug room, shut in from the cold mist outside, a bright fire burning, the furniture and utensils shining from laborious polishing, and a pipe and a flagon close at hand. These, then, are the kind of scenes which will meet us most frequently in studying the works of Dutch genre painting. The visit of the dentist, or the doctor, is another subject which shares the popularity of the ale-bench, the travelling musician, or the kitchen.

Jan Livens,* who was born at Leyden in 1607, was the son
of Lieven Hendrikse, a carpet manufacturer. He first studied
under Joris van Schooten at Leyden, and then is said to have
been a pupil under Lastman at the same time as Rembrandt,
whose influence is to be seen in his works. In 1630 Livens
was in England, painting the portraits of Charles I., his family,
and chief courtiers. On his return he settled in Antwerp,
where he became free of the Guild in 1635, and of the city five
years later. In 1661 he entered the Guild of Painters at the
Hague, but died at Antwerp in 1663. "His treatment of
sacred subjects is thoroughly *genre;* his sense of beauty, as
regards form, is not higher than that of Rembrandt; while in
depth of feeling, and power and warmth, as well as harmony of
colour, he stands far below him. On the other hand, he is
a better draughtsman" (Kugler's 'Handbook'). Works by
Livens are rather rare in public galleries. A *Study of a Head*
(Rotterdam Museum), a *Visitation* (in the Louvre), and a
Portrait of Joost van den Vondel, the poet (Amsterdam Gallery),
and *Abraham blessing Jacob,* are among the best. A remarkable picture, *The Raising of Lazarus,* by Livens, was exhibited
by the Baroness North in the collection of Old Masters at the
Royal Academy in 1871.

Adriaen Brouwer † was born, probably at Oudenaerde,‡
about 1605. Like his master Hals, he has suffered much at the
hands of his biographers, who have represented him as a
drunkard and the companion of drunkards. Though recent
research has not brought many facts to light concerning his life,
yet it has done sufficient to prove that he was not quite so bad
as Houbraken and Descamps would have us think. Brouwer
studied under Hals at Haarlem; then painted at Amsterdam,

* Or Lievens or Lievensz.
† It is sometimes written "de Brauwere" or "Brauwer," but the form
given above is the most correct.
‡ Haarlem is by some considered to be his birthplace.

FIG. 62.—ABRAHAM BLESSING JACOB. BY LIVENS.

and subsequently Antwerp, where he was received into the Painters' Guild in 1631, and also, in 1634, into the Society of Artists known as the "The Violet." He died at Antwerp in 1638, and was buried in the church of the Carmelites.

Brouwer seems to have delighted in painting scenes of riot and drunkenness in which he himself took part (Fig. 63). His power of colour is wonderful, and won for him the admiration of Rubens. His pictures are few and scarce. In the Munich Gallery we find, *Peasants playing Cards; Spanish Soldiers throwing Dice,* and another picture of the same class, and one of his best, *Card-Players Fighting.* The *Surgeon removing the Plaster,* in the same collection, is a wonderful work; the agonized expression of the patient writhing under the hand of the stolid doctor is perfectly life-like.

GERARD TER BORCH * stands first among a class of *genre* painters who, forsaking scenes of low life, painted the higher ranks of society. Ter Borch, who was born at Zwolle in 1608, studied art under his father, and at Haarlem; and afterwards visited Germany, Italy, and France; but without losing his originality. In 1648 he was at Münster, where the plenipotentiaries of Philip IV. of Spain and the delegates of the Dutch United Provinces were met to sign the treaty of peace. It was then that he painted his famous picture, the *Peace of Münster,* (signed " G. T. Borch,") now in the National Gallery, which contains portraits of the various persons assembled to ratify the treaty. Ter Borch was patronized and knighted by Philip IV., whose court he visited. He also visited the courts of France and England; and finally died at Deventer in 1681. The National Gallery contains another picture by this master, *The Guitar Lesson.* Ter Borch's *specialité* was the painting of a white satin dress, by which the chief light in his pictures is formed. Examples of this peculiarity of his style may be seen

* Or Terborch; the common form " Terburg " is wrong. His signature, when it does occur, is usually " G. T. Borch."

FIG. 63.—THE TOPERS. BY ADRIAEN BROUWER.

in *The Letter* (Fig. 64), (The Hermitage); *Paternal Advice* * (Amsterdam Museum), and a *Lady in a Satin Gown* (Dresden Gallery). Other notable pictures by Ter Borch are, the *Music Lesson*, and the *Officier Galant* (Louvre).

ADRIAAN JANSZ, commonly called VAN OSTADE,† was the son of one Jan Hendriex of Eyndhoven Adriaan was born in 1610 at Haarlem, where his parents had settled. He entered the studio of Frans Hals, and was there a fellow-pupil with Adriaen Brouwer. On leaving Hals he set up as a painter in Haarlem, where he was made Dean of the Guild in 1662, and lived and laboured until his death in 1685. Van Ostade has been styled the Rembrandt of *genre* painters. His subjects are similar to those of Teniers; indeed, he has been characterized as "a familiar Rembrandt, and a serious Teniers." But Van Ostade differs from Teniers as Rembrandt differed from Rubens: Teniers lavishes light everywhere, like Rubens; Van Ostade concentrates it, like Rembrandt. There is no beauty in Van Ostade's faces; his children are dwarfed and ugly, and he frequently shows us the grim side of peasant life in his pictures; but poetry is given by the glowing chiaroscuro, and by the sheer simplicity and *naïveté* of the treatment. He may be studied in the following works with advantage: The *Rural Concert* (Madrid), where some choristers are accompanied by a bagpipe, a broom-handle, and a mewing cat; three of the *Five Senses*, a valuable series, at St. Petersburg;

---

* Similar pictures are in the Berlin Gallery and at Bridgwater House, London : and a study for it in the Dresden Gallery.

† The sobriquet Van Ostade was adopted by the children of Jan at various times. We find it mentioned first in connection with Adriaan in 1636, when he was recorded as a member of the Civic guard. The name Ostade was derived from a small hamlet of that name (now called Ostedt), probably the birthplace of their father, near Eyndhoven. As Adriaan signed himself "Van Ostade" (or in early life "Ostaden") on almost all his works it has, not unnaturally, been looked upon as a surname.

FIG. 64.—THE LETTER. BY TER BORCH.
In the Hermitage, St. Petersburg

a *Smoking Scene*, and a *Painter's Studio* in a garret (Fig. 65), containing a portrait of himself, signed and dated 1663 (Dresden Gallery); a *Dutch Ale-house*, with fighting peasants (Munich); an *Old Man in His Study* (Rotterdam); a *Village Assembly* (Amsterdam); and the *Interior and Exterior* of a rustic house (The Hague). In the Louvre, Van Ostade has, in *His Family*, left ten wonderful portraits of Dutch faces. In the National Gallery we have one picture, the *Alchymist* (1661), by him; the Dulwich Gallery possesses four.

ISACK JANSZ, VAN OSTADE, was born at Haarlem in 1621, and was the younger brother and pupil of Adriaan van Ostade. He, too, adopted the name Van Ostade, and so signed himself. Little is known of his life. He died at Haarlem in 1649 (some say 1657). He was inferior to his brother in the figures of his *genre* pictures, but in out-of-door scenes (Fig. 66), especially in his favourite subject of a frozen canal with skaters, he stands alone. His pictures are comparatively rare in foreign galleries; England, which first brought Isack van Ostade's merits into notice, possesses most of the works of his short life in her private collections. In the Louvre is the *Halt of a Carrier*, refreshing himself outside a tavern, and an open Dutch landscape. There, too, is one of the numerous pictures of a *Frozen Canal*. Two of these frost-scenes, and a *Man in a Village Street*, are in the National Gallery.

BARTHOLOMEUS VAN DER HELST occupies the position of one of the best portrait-painters of this time, especially as producing a number of portraits in one picture. Almost nothing is known of his life, or teachers; but his works suggest the influence of Frans Hals. He was born, it is thought, in 1613, at Haarlem, where he passed his youth. He is supposed to have studied under Pynas, and Hals has also been mentioned as his instructor in art. In 1636 he was settled at Amsterdam, where he was the principal portrait painter, and received larger sums than Rembrandt for his paintings. He died in that city

FIG. 65.—ADRIAAN VAN OSTADE IN HIS WORKSHOP. BY HIMSELF.
In the Dresden Gallery.

FIG. 66.—THE COAST OF SCHEVELING. BY ISACK VAN OSTADE

FIG. 67.—THE BANQUET OF THE CIVIC GUARD. BY VAN DER HELST.
In the Amsterdam Museum.

in 1670.   It is in the Museum of Amsterdam we must look for
the principal pictures of Van der Helst. Here is his master-piece,
the *Banquet of the Civic Guard* (*de Schutters-maaltijd*),(Fig. 67),
which occupies a place of honour opposite to Rembrandt's *Night
Watch*. It is dated 1648. "The chief charm of this work
consists in the strong and truthful individuality of every part,
both in form and colour; in the capital drawing, which is
especially conspicuous in the hands; in the powerful and clear
colouring; and finally, in a kind of execution which observes
a happy medium between decision and softness" (Kugler's
'Handbook').   Sir Joshua Reynolds said of this work: "This
is, perhaps, the first picture of portraits in the world, com-
prehending more of those qualities which make a perfect portrait
than any other I have ever seen."   In the Amsterdam Museum
there are also other works by Van der Helst; notably a portrait
of the *Princess Mary*, daughter of Charles I. of England.   The
Rotterdam Museum among others has portraits of a *Man and
his Sister*, dated 1646, and of a *Cavalier and a Lady;* and our
National Gallery possesses a *Lady Studying*.

GERARD DOU was a clever pupil of Rembrandt, but not a
follower.   He was born at Leyden in 1613, and was apprenticed by his father, Douwe Janszoon de Vries van Arentsvelt, to
Bartholomeus Dolendo, the engraver, and in 1624 to Pieter
Kouwenhoven, the painter on glass.   From this narrow sphere
of art he emerged, and at the age of fifteen entered the studio
of Rembrandt.   Three years later Gerard Dou was an independent painter.   But few details are known of Dou's life.
With the exception of two gaps—of from 1651 to 1657, and
again from 1668 to 1672—he resided in his native city, where
he died in 1675.   Dou began by painting portraits, but
afterwards adopted the anecdotal style of art; and soon stood at
the head of a school of artists who made the infinitesimally little
their aim and object.   Some critics have said that the ideas of
Dou were as small as his subjects; but this is scarcely just.   He

did, indeed, delight to depict a broom-stick, or a woman scraping a carrot ; but then he painted broom-sticks and scraped-carrots as no one else could. He made his own brushes, pounded his

FIG. 68.—THE BUNCH OF GRAPES. BY DOU.

own colours, prepared his varnishes, panels, and canvas, with his own hands. He is said to have worked in a study opening on to a wet ditch, to avoid the dust. At Leyden, Dou was highly esteemed ; and the President, Van Spiring at the Hague, offered him 1000 florins a year for the right of making the first bid for his pictures. Dou's best work is the *Woman Sick of the Dropsy* (1663), in the Louvre ; the *Evening School* (Museum of Amsterdam) may be ranked next to it. Dou was fond of painting scenes in which the dentist, the doctor, or the quack plays a part; specimens of this kind are *The Empiric* (St. Petersburg), the *Chartalan on his Stage* (Munich). Dou frequently painted his own portrait ; one of these portraits is at Bridgwater House, another in the National Gallery. There, too, we have a *Portrait of Dou's Wife,* and the *Poulterer's Shop.*

FRANS VAN MIERIS was born at Delft in 1635. He studied under Gerard Dou, who called him the " prince of his scholars." He afterwards entered the studio of Abraham Tempel ; but it is Dou's influence which is always seen in his work. Van Mieris even surpassed his teacher in his careful elaboration of minute subjects. He might have been a draper from the accurate knowledge of silks, satins, and velvets, which he displays. His pictures are full of careless, happy, good-humoured life, like most of those of the Dutch School ; there is no emotion, no feeling in his works; the outside is admirably depicted, but it is nothing but outside. Among the best pictures by Van Mieris are a *Doctor feeling a Lady's pulse,* of the year 1656 (Belvedere, Vienna), a *Lady Fainting* in the presence of the doctor (Munich Gallery), *The Tinker* (Fig. 69), (Dresden Gallery), a *Boy blowing soap-bubbles,* dated 1663 (The Hague), a similar work is at Buckingham Palace. In the National Gallery, which is not rich in Dutch masters, is a picture of a *Lady in a crimson jacket*. Almost nothing is known of his life ; he died at Leyden in 1681.

WILLEM VAN MIERIS (1662—1747) imitated his father, Frans, very successfully. He was born, lived, and died at Leyden. His *Fish and Poultry-Shop,* signed and dated 1713 in the National Gallery, is a fair specimen of his art.

FIG. 69.—THE TINKER. BY FRANS VAN MIERIS.
In the Dresden Gallery.

GABRIEL METSU * was born in 1630 at Leyden, of parents who were both artists. He first studied under his father, Jan Metsu, a native of Belle, in Flanders, who was a painter of no great note; and then with Dou. He was admitted into the Guild of Painters at Leyden in 1648; but, leaving that city two years later, he went to Amsterdam, where he settled and probably spent the greater part of his life. In 1659 he received the right of citizenship of Amsterdam, where he died some time after 1667, the date of his last known work. He followed in the steps of Ter Borch and Gerard Dou; but made himself original by the freedom of his touch, and the power, richness, and harmony of his colours. We find the purple of the Van Eycks, and the silver of Paolo Veronese, in Metsu's pictures. Like Ter Borch, he preferred to delineate the upper classes in his pictures (Fig. 70); but he occasionally quitted the drawing-room for the kitchen or the market. In the Louvre we find Metsu well represented by the *Chemist*, the *Officer and Young Lady*, and especially by the *Vegetable Market at Amsterdam*. At Dresden are *The Lacemaker*, and the two *Poulterers*. In the Cassel Museum are *The Poulterer*, and the *Young Musician*. In the National Gallery we find three pictures by this master, two of which are *The Music Lesson*, and a *Duet*.

JAN HAVICKSZ STEEN was born at Leyden in 1626, the year following the marriage of his parents. His father, Havick Jansz Steen, who was in all probability a brewer, was of respectable family. The circumstances of Jan's life are enveloped in hopeless confusion. By some writers he is said to have been a brewer only, and not a keeper of an ale-house; by others, that he had a brewery is denied, while his ownership of an ale-house is upheld. And, again, the scene of his labours in various years is the subject of much controversy. Noticing the precocious talents of the young Jan, his father sent him to study under one Nicolas Knuffer (or Knupfer), a German painter of historical

* Sometimes written Metzu.

FIG. 70 —A DUTCH LADY PLAYING THE CLAVECIN. BY METSU.

subjects, settled at Utrecht. Jan then probably went to
Haarlem and entered the studio of Adriaan van Ostade, the
influence of whose style is, at any rate, perceptible in many of
his works. Adriaen Brouwer has, without sufficient reason, also
been mentioned among the names of his instructors in art.
Steen's last master was Van Goyen, of the Hague, whose
daughter, Margaretha, he married there in 1649; he had been
inscribed in the Painters' Guild at Leyden in the previous year.
Steen, it appears, was absent from Leyden from 1649 to 1653,
from 1653 to 1658, and from 1658 to 1672, during which
period many of his best works were painted. Perhaps some
years after 1649 were spent at the Hague. That he resided at
Haarlem at various times from 1661 to 1669 is more than
probable. In 1672 we find Steen back again at Leyden, and
in that year he applied for and obtained permission from the
magistrates to open a tavern, which he established at Langebrug.
In 1673 he married for a second time—his choice being Marie
van Egmont, widow of one Nicolas Herculens. In 1679, Jan
Steen died, and was buried in the parish church of St. Peter at
Leyden on the 3rd of February.

It has been the fashion to represent Jan Steen as a drunken,
roystering idler, never out of the ale-house. Like many others of
the Dutch masters, he has suffered from the misrepresentations of
biographers. As he has left upwards of five hundred pictures,
Steen must have been something more than a jovial, bibulous
landlord. He is, in fact, the laughing philosopher of Dutch art;
but the scenes of revelry and drunkenness which he painted
from the life in taverns, are not without their grim moral. In
this Steen somewhat resembles Hogarth, but without his stern
purpose; indeed, it has been well said that Jan Steen "is on
friendly terms with the devil even whilst painting his cloven
foot." Judging from Steen's portrait of himself at Amsterdam,
the laughter of the painter often covered a thoughtful mind or a
sad heart; and, like the melancholy clown, he made others laugh

FIG. 71.—THE PARROT'S CAGE. BY JAN STEEN.
In the Amsterdam Gallery.

without entering into the jest himself. Jan Steen's favourite
subjects were, besides the tavern drinking-bouts, bean-feasts,
and the like—a schoolmaster with a set of unruly boys ; a doctor
visiting a young girl; children in play or mischief; the sad
effects of intemperance ; or the folly of the alchemist seeking to
make gold. When he exerted himself, Jan Steen rivalled all
other *genre* painters of his country ; he is a master of expression,
and his best work is highly finished without triviality of execution ; but, perhaps from his habits of life, he was often careless.

At least two-thirds of Jan Steen's pictures are in the possession
of Englishmen. In the Northbrook collection is a *Portrait of
Steen* singing to his lute, and a *School*, a picture of a number of
schoolboys indulging in mischief whilst the fat pedagogue sleeps,
unconscious. In the National Gallery we must notice the *Music
Master ;* and in the Queen's collection at Buckingham Palace is
a picture of *The Toilet*, one of his most beautifully executed
works, remarkable for its clearness of colour and luminous quality.
In foreign galleries we find, in the Louvre, a *Flemish Festival*, the
usual ale-house scene; not one of the best specimens of this master,
nor of his school. At the Belvedere at Vienna there is a *Village
Wedding ;* at Berlin we may see *The Garden of an Alehouse ;*
and at the Hermitage, St. Petersburg, *The Game of Backgammon*
shows Jan Steen in his natural style—his own portrait is in the
picture ; whilst *Ahasuerus touching Esther with his golden
Sceptre*, exhibits the painter trying to treat a serious subject
seriously, and failing. At the Hague is the famous picture of
Human Life, which represents, oddly enough, about twenty
people, of all ages, engaged in eating oysters, hence it is sometimes called the *Oyster Feast*. In the same gallery is a picture
of *Steen and his family*. At Amsterdam there is a charming
picture in the best style of this master, called *The Feast of
St. Nicholas ;* where the good children are receiving toys, and
the naughty child finds a rod in his shoe. Here, and in the
picture representing the effects of intemperance,—in which

FIG. 72.—THE SOLDIER AND THE LAUGHING MAIDEN. BY VER MEER.
Formerly in the Double Collection, Paris

portraits of himself and his wife appear—Jan Steen gives us one of those brief, pointed lessons which no one could render better than himself.   In the Amsterdam Gallery, also, is his *Parrot's Cage* (Fig. 71), which, Kugler tells us, " exhibits a delicate taste in arrangement, a clearness and depth of warm tone approaching Ostade, and a solid execution."

JAN VER MEER,* of Delft, was born in that city in 1632. He is said to have studied under Karel Fabritius, and with Rembrandt at Amsterdam; but it is very doubtful if he ever had the advantage of Van Ryn's tuition.   He resided principally at Delft, where he probably died in 1696, for in that year a sale took place of twenty-one of his works.   Ver Meer adhered somewhat closely to Pieter de Hooch in his subjects and effects. His works are very scarce.   *The Soldier and the Laughing Maid* (Fig. 72) is an excellent example of his style.   In the Museum of the Hague we may see a *View of Delft*.   In the Six Collection at Amsterdam are two good specimens of this master's art—the *View of a Street*, probably in Delft, and a *Milk-Woman*. A *Lady playing a spinet*, a very fine painting, is in the possession of Her Majesty the Queen, at Windsor Castle.

CASPAR NETSCHER, though a German by birth, belongs distinctly to the Dutch School.   He was born at Heidelberg in 1639; studied art under Ter Borch at Deventer; and, after marrying at Bordeaux in 1659, established himself at the Hague, where he was elected a member of the Society of Painters in 1663.   He died in 1684.   He seems to have been very highly esteemed.   Charles II. invited him over to England, but he seems to have remained faithful to his adopted country, and to his art.   A glance at Netscher's pictures will suffice to show how thoroughly Dutch were his tastes and manner of treatment. The *Singing Lesson* and *Lesson on the Bass Viol* (both in the

* Commonly but incorrectly written Van der Meer.   He is not to be confounded with Van der Meer (or Ver Meer) of Haarlem, nor with Ver Meer of Utrecht.

Louvre); *Bathsheba*, dated 1667 (Munich), treated after the Dutch, and not after the Biblical, fashion; the *Suicide of Cleopatra* (Carlsruhe), where we see a Dutch woman very unlike the mistress of Roman Antony, are typical pictures by this master. He rivalled Ter Borch and Metsu in painting fabrics, especially in depicting goldsmith's work. We may study him in the National Gallery, where are three of his pictures—*Blowing*

FIG. 73.—THE SPINNER. BY NETSCHER.

Bubbles (1670), *Maternal Instruction,* and *The Spinner* (Fig. 73).

PIETER VAN SLINGELAND, who was born at Leyden in 1640, was a pupil of Gerard Dou; he painted with the greatest patience and laborious minuteness, and is said to have occupied three years in covering one square foot of canvas. His works are seldom seen in England. Indeed he only produced thirty pictures during his lifetime, which fact is not remarkable, as he took a whole month to paint a lace band. The *Dutch Family* (Louvre) is one of his most important works. He lived and laboured at Leyden, where he died in 1691.

GODFRIED SCHALCKEN, who was born at Dordrecht in 1643, was another pupil of Dou, and made his fame by candle-light effects. In the National Gallery we find, amongst others, *Lesbia*

FIG. 74.—THE VIOLIN PLAYER. BY EGLON VAN DER NEER.

weighing jewels against her sparrow. At Amsterdam is a candle-light *Portrait of William III.* His pictures are also to be found in the galleries of Vienna, Munich, and Dresden. He visited England, but worked chiefly at Dordrecht and at the Hague, where he died in 1706.

EGLON VAN DER NEER—who was born at Amsterdam in 1643,

was appointed Court Painter to Charles II. of Spain in 1687, and died at Düsseldorf in 1703—studied under his father, Artus van der Neer; but took for his models the works of Mieris and Netscher. He also painted historical works and landscapes, but they are less successful than his pictures of ladies playing the lute, and similar subjects, in which he delighted (Fig. 74).

PIETER DE HOOCH,* the son of Thomas Pietersz, a painter, was born at Ouderschie, a suburb of Rotterdam, about 1632. He worked at Delft, where he married Jannettje van der Burch in 1654; and a son was christened in the following year, and a daughter was baptized in 1656. In 1655 he was received, as a stranger, into the guild of St. Luke at Delft, but he appears to have left the city towards the close of 1657. Van der Willigen tells us that he went to Haarlem and died there in 1681; but Havard (in 'L'Art et les Artistes Hollandais,' III. 1880, in which he gives much that is new concerning this artist) denies that he went to Haarlem, and moreover states that dates on his pictures prove that he lived later than 1681. So little was this master known for a long time, that, although he even rivals Rembrandt in his wonderful *light* effects, his signature was frequently effaced from pictures, and some better known name inserted. In the effect produced by a ray of sunlight crossing a room no one, except Rembrandt, has equalled De Hooch, and not even he has surpassed him. In depicting the poetry of the fire-side, or the simple beauty of home life, this master is as great as Ter Borch or Metsu. *The Lace-maker* (Fig. 75), (Hermitage); *The Dutch Cabin* (Munich); and the *Buttery-Hatch* (Amsterdam Gallery), the last lighted by the sunbeam, are excellent specimens of De Hooch's work. The *Card Party* (Buckingham Palace); Two *Courtyards*, one *Interior* (National Gallery), as well as several pictures in private collections, represent in England this artist, whose works are scarce even in his own country.

* Or Hooche, Hooghe, Hoogh, or Hooge.

FIG. 75.— THE LACE-MAKER. BY PIETER DE HOOCH.
In the Hermitage, St. Petersburg.

ADRIAAN VAN DER WERFF, who was born at Kralingen, near Rotterdam, in 1659, studied under one Cornelis Picolett and with Eglon van der Neer. He died at Rotterdam in 1722. He stands alone in the Dutch School of this period as a painter of historical and mythological pieces, instead of the favourite subjects of his brethren. His pictures show a yearning after the *ideal* which he could never reach. Still his works were most eagerly sought after, and from the Elector Palatine downwards, Van der Werff's studio was thronged by patrons. His sacred subjects lack the dignity which should belong to them. A picture of the *Elector Palatine and his Consort*, surrounded by allegorical figures of the Arts (Munich Gallery), illustrates two of this master's peculiarities, the union of coldness and want of taste with wonderful workmanship. A sacred picture, *Ecce Homo* (Munich Gallery), displays the ivory-like hue of the flesh which is one of Van der Werff's characteristics. His works are not popular in England, but in Buckingham Palace we find a picture of *Lot and his daughters*, of singular warmth of colouring, a *Boy with a sucking pig*, and *Girl with a kitten*.

CORNELIS DUSART was born at Haarlem in 1660; entered the Guild there in 1679, and died there in 1704. He studied under Adriaan van Ostade, and imitated him successfully. His works are found in the best foreign galleries, and in many private collections in England. The *Fish Market* and the *Village Inn* may be seen in the Amsterdam Gallery.

CHAPTER III.

LANDSCAPE painting is the creation of the Netherlands. Even Carracci, Domenichino, and Poussin merely used a landscape as the theatre for some historical subject or human drama. It was Pauwel Bril of Antwerp, who, half a century before Claude Lorrain, invented landscape painting pure and simple. It is natural that the Dutch masters, who made Nature in her varying aspects their special study, should cultivate landscape painting as an especial branch of their art. Among the earliest who cultivated this kind of painting we must place—

JAN VAN GOYEN, who, though his colouring is monotonous, was one of the best landscape painters of this time. He was born at Leyden in 1596 ; studied under Isack van Swanenburgh, Jan de Man, and Willem Gerritz ; and then went to Haarlem, and became influenced by the style of Esajas van de Velde. He worked at Leyden and at the Hague, where he died in 1656. In the Amsterdam Gallery we find, amongst others, a *View on the Meuse* (Fig. 76), and the *Castle of Valkenhof* by him. Amongst other pupils, he taught Berchem and Jan Steen, who, as we have seen, afterwards became his son-in-law.

FIG. 76.—THE BANKS OF THE MAAS. BY VAN GOYEN.

In the Amsterdam Gallery.

JAN WYNANTS commences the school of real Dutch land-scape painters. For him the flat scenery of his native Holland possessed charms which he was never tired of depicting. With Wynants and his successors Nature is no more the theatre for a subject. In his pictures we find as a rule a winding road, apparently starting from nowhere, and leading nowhither, whilst a few figures and animals are introduced by the hands of assist-ants and cotemporary artists. Wynants may be studied in England, at Dresden, Munich, Paris, Amsterdam, and the Hague. At Dresden are two *Landscapes* with figures. At the Hague is one of his last landscapes, dated 1675. There are five of his pictures in the National Gallery, and two in the Dulwich Gallery. Truthfulness to nature is the chief characteristic of Wynants; this is seen in aërial perspective, and in the leaves of plants (Fig. 77). His tints are clear and bright, especially in the blue-green of his trees and plants. Wynants painted at Haarlem; but details of his life are entirely wanting. The latest date on any of his works, 1679, is seen on a *Landscape with figures*, by him, in the Hermitage, St. Petersburg.

AELBERT CUYP, the son and pupil of Jacob Gerritsz Cuyp, a portrait painter of note, was born at Dordrecht in 1605. He lived, as a rule, on his own estate of Dordwijk, near Dordrecht, in which city he died in 1691. He has been justly named " the Dutch Claude." But it was not only as a landscape painter that he was famous. He painted a number of portraits, and with fair success. He painted also fruit, flowers, and dead game, but with-out equalling the greatest masters of this branch of art. His scenes of Interiors are executed in the manner of Van Ostade and Teniers, as, for example, the *Mussel-eater*, in the Rotterdam Museum. His interiors of buildings have never been surpassed, not even by Emanuel de Witte. He painted animals in a way which made him the model of Paul Potter, though unlike him he never sacrifices the landscape to the animals. But above all Cuyp is famous for his animated landscapes, and scenes on the

FIG. 77.—THE OLD CASTLE. BY WYNANTS.

banks of rivers. He is the greatest lover of light, except Rembrandt, of all the Dutch masters. No painter has ever expressed more truthfully the light warmth of a misty summer's day, such as Cuyp had often experienced on the banks of the Maes, or in the streets of his native Dordrecht. Strangely enough Cuyp was not appreciated in Holland till it was too late, and most of his works had left that country before men learned to value them. In the Dulwich Gallery there are fourteen works by Cuyp, and there are eight in the National Gallery, among which is the fine *Landscape, with Cattle and Figures; Evening* (Fig. 78), signed A;Cuijp. The love of light which this master displayed is seen even in a night scene, the *Banks of a Lake*, at Grosvenor House. One of his finest pictures is a *View of the Maese near Dordrecht*, in the Bridgwater Gallery, unrivalled for the flood of golden sunset light with which the picture glows; another equally beautiful work represents the same favourite scene, and is at Dorchester House. There is an excellent specimen of his powers as a portrait painter in the National Gallery.

CORNELIS DECKER, who entered the Guild at Haarlem in 1643, and died in poverty in that city in 1678, was a landscape painter of the same school as Ruisdael, to whom Decker's works were for a long time attributed.

JAN BOTH and ANDRIES BOTH, were two brothers who lived in the early half of the seventeenth century. Jan was born at Utrecht about 1610, and Andries a little earlier. Though the former was the younger, he was the more important of the two. We find that Andries devoted the greater part of his time to the painting of figures in Jan's landscapes, and works by his own hands entirely are consequently rarely to be met with. They both studied first under their father Dirk Both, a painter on glass, and subsequently became pupils of Abraham Bloemart. We learn that they travelled together to Italy, and were influenced by the paintings of Claude Lorrain. In their land-

FIG. 78.—LANDSCAPE, WITH CATTLE AND FIGURES. BY CUYP.

In the National Gallery (No. 53).

scapes, therefore, we must look for Italian scenery rather than
that of Holland. Andries Both was drowned in a canal before
1644.* Jan resided chiefly at Utrecht, and was still living there
in 1662.† In the Hague Gallery are two good *Italian landscapes*, by the brothers. The *Artist studying from Nature* (Van
der Hoop Collection, Amsterdam) is their masterpiece. In
England the National Gallery has six works by Jan Both,
besides which there are several in private collections.

Another Dutch artist who drew his inspiration from Italy is
PIETER VAN LAAR, who was born in 1613 at Laaren, near
Naarden : he was called from his deformity BAMBOCCIO. After
living for sixteen years in Rome, he returned to Holland, and
settled at Haarlem, where he died in 1674. His landscapes
show the influence of Claude and Poussin. His pictures, which
are very rare, are to be found in the Galleries of Florence, Cassel,
Dresden, Vienna, and Paris.

AART VAN DER NEER was a landscape painter, who remained
faithful to his native Holland in his choice of subjects. He
was essentially the poet-painter of the night, and his leading
characteristic is a certain mysterious twilight effect. In the
National Gallery is a *Landscape*, with the figures and cattle
added by Cuyp, who has signed his name on a pail. There,
too, are to be found a *River Scene*, and a *Canal Scene*. Van
der Neer may be studied in the Berlin Gallery where there
are eight of his works; he is found in many private collections
in England and abroad. Details of Van der Neer's life are
entirely wanting. He was born, it is thought, in 1619 at
Amsterdam, where he chiefly resided, and where he is said to
have died in 1683.

---

* Not 1650, as usually given.

† In this year an engraved portrait of him was published in ' *Het
Guldencabinet*' at Antwerp : it bears the following inscription, "Jean
Both, good and well-respected landscape-painter, staying now at Utrecht,
his native town" (*see Dulwich Gallery Catalogue, by Dr. J. P. Richter*).

FIG. 79.—THE FISH-SELLER. BY WOUWERMAN.

PHILIPS WOUWERMAN * is a painter of whose life little is
known. He was born at Haarlem in 1619. He first studied
his father Paulus Joosten Wouwerman, an historical painter of
no great note ; he then entered the studio of Wynants ; and
after that, he made, at the early age of nineteen, a run-away
marriage at Hamburg, where he studied under Evert Decker.
Returning to Haarlem, he entered the Guild in 1640, and lived
in comfortable circumstances until his death in 1668. With
regard to his works, Ruskin speaks of them with contempt,† and
laughs at the various discordant elements which are introduced
into one picture. Kugler, on the other hand, says : " His
compositions invariably evince a delicate feeling for the pictur-
esque ; his figures and animals are well drawn and full of
animation . . . . . His general keeping is singularly tender ;
his touch unites great finish with equal delicacy and spirit.''
And Lord Ronald Gower thus speaks of his works—" paintings
in which it is not easy to know which most to admire, whether
the beauty of their composition and grouping, the brilliancy and
clear tone of their colouring, or their wonderful variety."
Wouwerman must have been a master of vast industry, and of
great rapidity of execution, since he declared that his pictures
required two leagues of gallery for their reception. Like Holbein,
however, Wouwerman has had a great number of works falsely
attributed to him ; some of them may have been painted by his
brothers Pieter and Jan. It has been a common mistake to
insist that every Dutch picture in which a white horse is conspicuous, must of necessity be the work of Wouwerman. He
chiefly painted battle-pieces and landscapes, in which are figures
of horses and dogs accompanying their masters (Fig. 79).

Of the many hundred pictures attributed to Wouwerman
there are in the Dresden Gallery sixty-six (of which about
sixty are considered genuine), in the Hermitage fifty, twenty-

---

* Wouverman, Wouwermans, and several other forms are found.

† But Mr. Ruskin has expressed his wish that all the pictures of the
Dutch School might be burnt.

FIG. 80.—THE YOUNG BULL. BY PAULUS POTTER.

In the Gallery at the Hague,

three at Cassel, about seventeen at Munich, thirteen in the
Louvre, ten in Buckingham Palace, eight in the National Gallery,
and nine in the Dulwich Gallery, besides others scattered in
various places.   Wornum declares, however, that we should
place the number of genuine pictures by Wouwerman at about
ninety instead of nine hundred.   At the Louvre we may notice
the *Bœuf gras*, the *Riding School*, and two *Cavalry Scenes*.
At Dresden there are some excellent hunting scenes, *Stag-
hunts, Heron-hunting*, etc.   At St. Petersburg we find the
Burning Mill and the *Flemish Carousal*.   At the Hague is a
superb landscape known as the *Chariot de foin*, and a great
Battle-piece, similar in composition to the work, well-known as
the *Battle of Nördlingen*, in the Munich Gallery.

JAN FRANS VAN BREDAEL, a native of Antwerp (1683—1750),
was a pupil and follower of Wouwerman.   He was also influenced by the works of Velvet Brughel, as in his *View of a Village* (Fig. 98) in the Amsterdam Gallery.   Other works by him
are in the Dresden Gallery and the Louvre.

PAULUS POTTER stands at the head of the Dutch painters
who introduced animals into their pictures.   He has been
styled the "Raphael of animals," but he scarcely deserves the
name, as his object was accuracy of detail, not beauty, in his
delineations of the herd.   Paul Potter, who was born at
Enkhuizen in 1625, was instructed in art by his father, Pieter
Simonsz Potter,* a landscape painter.   He is said to have also
studied under Jacob de Wet, at Haarlem.   He lived for some
time with his father at Amsterdam, then went to Delft, where he
was received into the Guild in 1646, and there painted many of
his best pictures.   In 1649 he settled at the Hague, for a time,
and his genius commanded universal respect.   He returned, in
1652, to Amsterdam, where he died of over-work in 1654.

At the Hague is the famous picture which Paul Potter painted
when only twenty-two—*The Young Bull* (Fig. 80).   The picture

* A *Stag-Hunt* by him is in the National Gallery.

represents a landscape in which are assembled a young bull, a cow, three sheep, and the shepherd, all of life-size. In this somewhat over-rated work, Paul Potter displays a new system of his own creation, or rather the union of two systems. He first painted the picture in the manner of the great hunting scenes of Snyders, with a strong and deep impasto in the masses ; then over this he traced

FIG. 81.—CATTLE. FROM AN ETCHING BY PAULUS POTTER.

the details, as finely finished as a house by Van der Heyden, or a face by Denner. *The Bear-hunt* (Amsterdam Museum) is an unpleasant picture, which abundantly proves how inferior Potter's large-proportioned figures were to his smaller ones. In London there are two of his master-pieces, *Cows and Sheep* in a land-scape under willow trees, in the possession of the Duke of

Westminster, and a *Country Scene,* in the possession of the
Queen at Buckingham Palace.   The National Gallery has a
Landscape with Cattle, of the year 1651, and another work
called *The Old Grey Hunter.*   In St. Petersburg Paul Potter is
better represented than in his own country, or in England.
There we may see the wonderful polyptych representing the trial
of man by the animals ; the two central panels shows us the

FIG. 82.—PEASANTS. A DRAWING BY BERGHEM.
Formerly in the Periere Collection.

Condemnation of Man by the Tribunal of Animals.   There also
we must notice a *Huntsmen Halting,* dated 1650, and above all
The Cow of the previous year, which is considered one of his
masterpieces.   In this latter picture the painter has introduced
into his landscape cows, horses, asses, sheep, hens, a cat and dog,
as well as human figures.   There are admirable etchings of animals
by this artist (Fig. 81).

NICOLAAS (or CLAAS, the shortened form) PIETERSZ is commonly known as BERCHEM * (or Berghem). He was born at Haarlem in 1620, and received his first instruction in art from his father, Pieter Claasz van Haarlem. He afterwards studied under Jan van Goyen, N. Moeyaert, De Grebber, and Jan Wils, whose daughter he married, and with Weenix. The pictures he painted in early life have some resemblance to the works of Weenix, and, like them, represent seaports and embarkations. He afterwards formed for himself a different and more interesting manner, representing landscapes and most delightful scenery, enriched with architectural ruins and decorated with charming groups of figures and cattle. He occasionally painted animals in the works of other masters, as Ruisdael, Hobbema, and Jan Wils. In the Museum of Amsterdam there are a *Ruth and Boaz* and other works; a *Cavalry Combat* is in the Hague Gallery; and in the Louvre he is well represented by a *View of Nice*, the *Port of Genoa*, a *Ford*, and *Cattle drinking;* while in the National Gallery are five good examples of his style, and at Dulwich six. His pictures tell us that Berchem visited Italy, but there is no further record on the subject. He died at Amsterdam in 1683.

ALDERT VAN EVERDINGEN, who was born at Alkmaar in 1621, studied, it is said, under Roelandt Savery and Pieter Molyn. While on a voyage to the Baltic, he was shipwrecked on the Norwegian shore, where the rugged beauty of the coast made an everlasting impression on his mind. As if in contrast to the artist-travellers who brought back Italy with them to Holland, Aldert van Everdingen, bringing back from his travels the mountainous scenes of Norway, shadowed with firs, and intersected with ravines and waterfalls, introduced into Dutch painting the nature of the extreme north. He died at Amsterdam in

---

* By several writers this has been assumed to be a mere nickname; but inasmuch as he is entered in the town records as Berchem, and that he so signed his works, it may to all intents and purposes be considered a surname.

1675. A *Norwegian Landscape* by him, in the Amsterdam
Gallery, is a good example of his style, and the Dresden Gallery
has five works by him. Van Everdingen deserves greater praise
as an engraver than as a painter ; the British Museum possesses
a good collection of his prints.   A version of 'Reineke Fuchs'
with fifty-seven engravings from the original plates, by Van
Everdingen, was published in England in 1843 (Fig. 83).

FIG. 83.—PREPARATIONS FOR A PILGRIMAGE. BY VAN EVERDINGEN.
From Reynard the Fox.

KAREL DU JARDIN * was born at Amsterdam (?) about 1625.
He was a pupil of Berchem, and was influenced by the style of
Potter.   He visited Rome at an early age, and became imbued
with a taste for Italian scenes.   He returned through Lyons,
where he married, to Holland, in 1656, and having joined the
Guild at the Hague, settled at Amsterdam.   In 1669 he returned
to Italy, and lived there till his death, at Venice, in 1678.   In

* Or Dujardin.

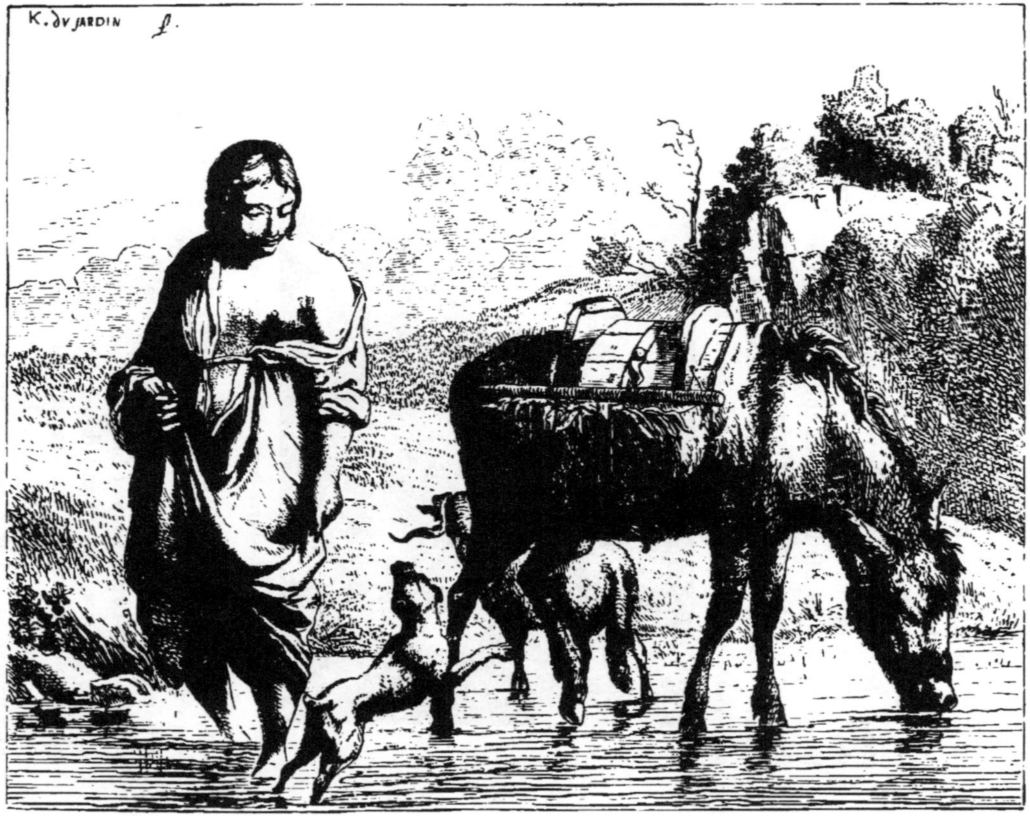

Fig. 84.—The Ford. By Du Jardin.

painting animals Du Jardin imitates the style of Paul Potter. In the Amsterdam Museum we find, among other works by Du Jardin, a *Mounted Trumpeter*, and a *Peasant winnowing corn*. Sacred subjects are beyond his grasp, as, for example, the *Calvary* in the Louvre, which collection is, however, rich in better works by his hand. In the National Gallery there are four works by this painter: *Figures and Animals reposing* (1656); *Fording the Stream* (1657); a *Landscape with Cattle*; and *Sheep and Goats*, of the year 1673, when he must have been in Italy.

FIG. 85.—RIVER-SCENE. BY SALOMON RUYSDAEL.

As a portrait painter Du Jardin was not without merit, though somewhat cold in tone. He is best seen in that branch of art in the Amsterdam Gallery, where are *His own Portrait* (of the year 1662), that of his patron, *G. Reijnst*, and *Portraits of five Syndics*, signed and dated 1669. He executed many admirable etchings of landscapes with cattle (Fig. 84).

SALOMON VAN RUYSDAEL was born, about 1600, at Haarlem, and was admitted as a master into the Guild there in 1623. Haarlem, with its immediate neighbourhood, was the scene of

FIG. 86.—THE RUSTIC BRIDGE. BY JACOB VAN RUISDAEL.

most of his labours.   He died in 1670.   He was a pupil of Van
Goyen, and his landscapes are not without merit ; but his fame
has been surpassed by that of his nephew Jacob.   He is best
seen in the galleries of Berlin and Dresden.   The former has
four works by him, and the latter three.

JACOB VAN RUISDAEL * stands at the head of Dutch landscape
painters. Born at Haarlem about 1625, and at first educated for
the practice of medicine, Ruisdael studied art under his uncle
Salomon, and perhaps also under Berchem.   He died in poverty
in the almshouses at Haarlem in 1682.

The works of Ruisdael are the embodiment of the poetry of
melancholy.   He painted the scenery of his own country, and
delighted to depict a wide stretch of land or water, darkened
by stormy clouds, or overhanging trees.   He was not successful
in painting men and animals, and sought the assistance of
his brethren in this branch of art.   He sometimes painted
views of a Norwegian character (Fig. 86), but it is not known
that he ever visited Norway.   Ruisdael is probably equalled,
or even surpassed in some technical points, by other Dutch
masters, but none have approached to the mystic melancholy
which invests his pictures. In the Louvre we find the *Coup
de Soleil*, and a *Storm*, the scene of which is on the coast
near the dykes of Holland.   Michelet calls this picture, "The
prodigy of the Louvre."   In Holland, we see amongst others
in the Amsterdam Museum, *The Waterfall*, and a *View of
Bentheim Castle.*   In England, Ruisdael's pictures are chiefly
in private collections.   The National Gallery, however, now
possesses twelve of his landscapes.   In the Hermitage at St.
Petersburg there are fourteen pictures by Ruisdael.   His
greatest works are, however, to be seen in Germany ; at Munich
there are nine landscapes, and among the fourteen of his
pictures at Dresden is the celebrated *Chase.*   Under the

* Or Ruijsdael ; but only his earlier works are signed in this manner
(*Dr. J. P. Richter*).

FIG. 87.—LANDSCAPE. BY HOBBEMA.
In Buckingham Palace.

wonderfully painted birch trees, Adriaan van de Velde has depicted a stag-hunt which gives the picture its name. At Vienna is the most important, and perhaps the most perfect, of Ruisdael's works; it is called *The Forest,* and is the truest and most excellent portrait of simple nature that can be imagined.

FRÉDÉRIC DE MOUCHERON, a landscape painter, was born at Embden in 1633, and studied under Asselyn at Amsterdam. Then he went to Paris, where he was very popular, and resided for some time. Returning to Holland, he settled in Amsterdam, and produced many good landscapes in which the figures were usually painted by Adriaan van de Velde and Lingelbach. Moucheron is said to have died at Amsterdam in 1686, but a *Garden Scene,* in the Dresden Gallery, signed and dated 1713, if genuine, disproves this statement. Landscapes by Moucheron are in the Gallery at the Hague, in the Van Loon Collection at Amsterdam, and in the National Gallery. He executed numerous water-colour drawings remarkable for delicacy of drawing and tender colour; somewhat in the style of Claude, but rather overloaded with detail in the composition.

JAN HACKAERT, who was born at Amsterdam about 1636, studied first in his native town, and afterwards in Switzerland. He died at Amsterdam in 1699. He specially devoted himself to woodland scenery. Adriaan van de Velde and other artists painted the figures in Hackaert's pictures. A *Landscape with Dogs and Hunters* (Steengracht Collection at the Hague), is of great merit. A *Stag-hunt* is in the National Gallery.

MEINDERT HOBBEMA was cotemporary with Jacob van Ruisdael, and ranks next to him among the Dutch landscape painters. He was born at Amsterdam, in 1638, and there spent the greater part of his life. He died there in 1709. He probably resided for a time at Haarlem; and is said to have studied under Salomon van Ruysdael. He chose similar subjects to those of his great cotemporary, but as a rule painted sunlight scenes rather than the gloomy effects beloved of Jacob van Ruisdael. Hobbema

FIG. 88.—WINTER LANDSCAPE. BY ADRIAAN VAN DE VELDE.
In the Dresden Gallery.

was, during his life, and even long after his death, totally unappreciated in Holland. Now his pictures are of the greatest value, and command vast sums, whereas the painter died poor and neglected. In Holland we find Hobbema represented only at Rotterdam. In the Munich Gallery is a *Dutch Cabin ;* at Berlin a *Forest ;* in the National Gallery, *The Avenue, Middel-harnis,* and six other landscapes. Some of this master's best pictures are in private collections in England—such as those of Her Majesty the Queen (Fig. 87), Sir Richard Wallace, Mr. Holford, and Lord Overstone. Figures were introduced into Hobbema's paintings by Berchem, Adriaan van de Velde, Lingelbach, Philips and Pieter Wouwerman and other artists.

ADRIAAN VAN DE VELDE, born at Amsterdam in 1639, first studied under his father Willem van de Velde, the elder, and was then apprenticed to Wynants at Haarlem. He died in his native city in 1672. In addition to the calm, smiling landscapes which he painted so admirably, Adriaan van de Velde drew human figures nearly as well as Wouwerman, and animals in a manner which Paul Potter would not have despised. Peaceful pastoral scenes were his favourite subjects. The rustic Phyllis and some Dutch Corydon resting in the shade are the usual figures in his pictures. In the Louvre we find *The Coast of Scheveningen,* where the Prince of Orange appears in a carriage and six horses ; the *Frozen Canal,* the *Herdsman's Family,* and three landscapes with animals. The galleries of Dresden, Munich, Berlin, Rotterdam, the Hague, Amsterdam, and Antwerp, all contain good specimens of this master. The Van der Hoop Collection at Amsterdam contains one very notable work— *Portraits of Himself, his Wife, and his Two Children.* In the Dresden Gallery is a *Winter Landscape* (Fig. 88). There are six pictures by him in the National Gallery.

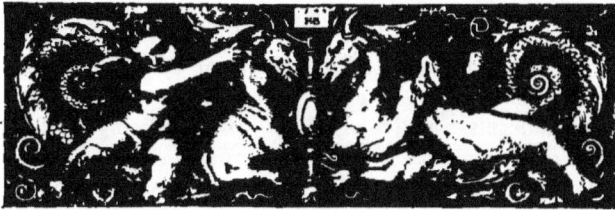

CHAPTER IV.

I T is natural that Holland, a country stolen from the sea, and at one time the rival of Britain in the sovereignty of the waves, should have produced some famous marine painters. As Holland possessed her De Ruyters and Van Tromps to manœuvre her ships and fight her battles, so she had also her Van de Veldes and Bakhuisens to paint them. One of the earliest of these painters is—

SIMON DE VLIEGER, who was born at Rotterdam about 1600, and was still living in 1656. His master is not known with certainty, but he doubtless studied under Jan van Goyen. He entered the Guild of Delft in 1634, and became a citizen of Amsterdam in 1643. De Vlieger combined the manner of Cuyp with the subjects of Van de Velde. He was the first painter who set himself to represent the sea in its various phases, now sleeping in calm, now lashed into fury by the tempest. His colouring is often unpleasing. In one of his earlier pictures, a *Sea Piece* (Hermitage, St. Petersburg), the effect is cold. In the Amsterdam Gallery is a *River Scene*, with the Admiral's yacht firing a salute, which is far more striking. *A Storm at Sea* (Munich Gallery), and a view of the *Coast of Scheveningen* (Bridgwater Gallery), are excellent speci·

ınens of De Vlieger's art. The etchings of this artist are varied and powerful.

JAN PARCELLIS, a native of Ghent, who was living in Haarlem in 1628, had the reputation there, perhaps a purely local one, of being "the best painter of ships in existence." His master-piece seems to be a sea-piece in the Schleissheim Gallery, dated 1629.

REMIGIUS NOOMS, called from his love of marine pictures ZEEMAN, was born at Amsterdam about 1616. Nothing is known of the life of this painter except what can be gathered from his etchings. These show that he was cotemporary with De Vlieger, and that he visited France and England. In his marine pictures he does not equal other painters of this school; but his ships are carefully and accurately drawn. His pictures are rare in public galleries. At Amsterdam there is a picture of a sea-fight between the English and Dutch fleets, near Leghorn; the galleries of Vienna and Cassel contain each a specimen of this artist, whose etchings, however, are better than his oil paintings.

JAN BEERESTRAATEN * is essentially a painter of Amsterdam. He was born there in 1622, painted there, and died there, it is sup-posed, in 1687; and it is in Amsterdam that his best works must be sought. From his works, however, we know that he visited Bois-le-Duc, Minden, Rotterdam, Haarlem, and Leyden; but it is not likely that he ever went to Italy, although he painted views of that country. His pictures are principally coast scenes and views in towns, with figures which were occasionally painted by Lingelbach. In the Amsterdam Gallery there is the *Boat-men's House, Amsterdam;* the *Ruins of the old Town-hall, Amster-dam;* and a *Sea-fight between the English and Dutch;* and he

---

* An Alexander Beerestraaten is mentioned by various writers on art as a brother of Jan; but M. Havard (in 'L'Art et les Artistes Hollandais') denies his existence, and considers Jan to be the author of those works attributed to Alexander.

is also well represented in the Town-hall, and in the Six and Van der Hoop collections. Jan Beerestraaten executed many paintings, and a large number of drawings. He was a good colourist, and selected pleasing subjects, but was wanting in firmness of execution.

FIG. 89.—A GALE. BY LUDOLF BAKHUISEN.

LUDOLF BAKHUISEN,* who was born at Emden in 1631, was at first intended for trade, and did not commence the study of art till after his eighteenth year. He was a pupil of Aldert van Everdingen at Amsterdam, and, it is said, also received instruction in art from Hendrik Dubbels. He died at Amster-

* Or Backhuijsen.

dam in 1708. Bakhuisen studied the details of every kind of vessel, and re-produced the rigging and other technicalities of the various craft with great accuracy. He is said also to have gone afloat in all weathers, that he might study the ocean in its many moods. In colour and in natural feeling, he is inferior to Willem van de Velde. Bakhuisen was a popular, successful painter, and had many royal and noble patrons. His most notable works are, the *Disembarkation of William III.* (the Hague); the *Embarkation of Jan de Witte on the Dutch Fleet* (Amsterdam); *View of the Port of Amsterdam* (Vienna); and *Dutch Shipping*, and *Off the Mouth of the Thames*, both in the National Gallery, where there are four other works by this master. Comparing Bakhuisen's dark and rather hard treatment with the transparency of Willem van de Velde, a critic says, "Backhuysen makes us fear the sea, Van de Velde makes us love it" (Fig. 89).

WILLEM VAN DE VELDE "the younger," the elder brother of Adriaan van de Velde, stands first among Dutch marine painters. He was born at Amsterdam in 1633, and studied first under his father, Willem van de Velde "the elder," but chiefly under Simon de Vlieger. Whilst in Holland, in his earlier life, he painted, among many other sea-pieces, several naval battles in which the Dutch were victorious over their English rivals. Subsequently he went with his father to England, and obtained in 1677 a salary of £100 a year from Charles II. for painting sea-fights of which his father had made draughts at a similar remuneration. Whilst in England, Van de Velde judiciously painted battles in which victory was on the side of the English. James II. continued the pension to the two Van de Veldes, the younger of whom died in London in 1707, and was buried beside his father in St. James's Church, Piccadilly.

By his constant study of nature, Van de Velde "the younger" has been able to present the sea in every phase of its many-sided temper, and always with equal success. In the technical

FIG. 90.—THE CALM. BY WILLEM VAN DE VELDE.

part of his work, he is most accurate, every rope being painted with care and study. These qualities made him the most popular of painters with the two chief maritime countries of the world, England and Holland; and it is in these two countries that the majority of his many pictures (of which 329 are enumerated) are to be found.

In the Amsterdam Museum are two pictures representing the battle between the Dutch fleet under De Ruyter and the English in 1666. The artist has depicted himself in a small boat; and it is a fact that he was actually present during the engagement sketching the scene. In the National Gallery are fourteen pictures by Van de Velde. Among private collections in England, that at Bridgwater House contains the best specimens —two *Naval Battles;* a *View on the Texel;* a *Calm; Entrance to the Bril;* and the *Rising of the Gale;* but the finest of his calm seas is perhaps the *Morning Gun,* a very large picture in the possession of Sir Richard Wallace.

JAN DUBBELS, a marine painter, of whose life nothing is known, has been described both as the master and the pupil of Bakhuisen. Many of his pictures have been wrongly attributed to that master. "His subjects were chiefly sea-coast scenes, which, for truth, mastery of keeping and aërial perspective, beauty of lighting, and breadth and softness of execution, may be placed on the same level with Ruysdael and Willem van de Velde. . . . . His chief work, signed with his name, and of considerable dimensions, is a *Sea-coast,* against which an agitated sea is breaking; in the Van der Hoop collection at Amsterdam. It is one of the finest sea-pieces in the whole Dutch school known to me" (Kugler's 'Handbook').

JAN VAN DE CAPELLE * is another painter of whose life we have no details. He received the freedom of Amsterdam in 1653. He clearly lived in the best period of his school; the dates on his works extend from 1650 to 1680. Like De

_____
* He sometimes wrote it Cappelle.

Vlieger, whom he much resembled, Van de Capelle blended the manner of Cuyp with the subjects of Van de Velde. There are five of his pictures in the National Gallery, and several others in private galleries. His favourite subject is a calm sea reflecting a light and sunny sky.

FIG. 91.—FROM AN ETCHING BY REMBRANDT.

CHAPTER V.

PAINTERS OF ARCHITECTURE AND STILL LIFE.

BEFORE speaking of the Dutch painters of still-life, in the proper sense of the term, we must notice some artists who devoted themselves to the painting of buildings. Among those who depicted the exteriors of buildings was—

EMANUEL MURAND, a native of Amsterdam in 1622, and a Pupil of Philips Wouwerman. He chose dilapidated farm-houses and Dutch villages as his special subjects. The careful exactness of the Dutch School is mainly manifest in his houses, where every brick and stone is minutely described. The works of Murand are most rare in public galleries. There is a dilapidated old *Farm-House* in the Amsterdam Museum; and a *Farm-yard with Cattle*, in the Museum of Rotterdam. Murand died at Leeuwarden in 1700.

JAN VAN DER HEYDE * was born at Gorcum in 1637, and first studied under a painter on glass, whose name has not been recorded. Leaving his native town he established himself at Amsterdam, where he soon rose to fame. He travelled in Belgium, the Rhine Provinces, and visited England. Van der Heyde produced many pictures during his long life, and would

* Frequently written Heyden.

doubtless have painted many more, had not his improvement in that very inartistic object, a fire-engine, gained for him in 1672 the post of director of the fire-brigade in Amsterdam. He died in that city in 1712. Van der Heyde has been called "the Gerard Dou of architectural painters." He combined in his pictures of buildings extreme minuteness of detail with a fine general effect; and his harmonious contrast of light and shadow gave a picturesqueness even to a stiff and formal street of houses. His favourite subjects were churches, palaces, and other public buildings in Holland and Belgium. Adriaan van de Velde painted many of the figures in Van der Heyde's pictures, and thus increased their beauty. After Van de Velde's death, Van der Neer and Lingelbach undertook this part of the work. Of Van der Heyde's works we may specially call attention to the *Amsterdam Town-hall* (The Louvre); *View of a Dutch town* (Amsterdam); *View of a public Square,* shaded by trees (Munich); *View of a Netherlandish town* (The Hague); and a *Street in Cologne* (National Gallery, where there are three other views by this artist). In the Dulwich Gallery there is a *View of two Churches and a Town-wall,* with figures by Adriaan van de Velde.

JOB BERCK-HEYDE *'was born at Haarlem in 1630; studied under Jacob de Wet, and entered the Painters' Guild in 1654. With his younger brother Gerrit, who from his pupil became his collaborator, he travelled through Germany and was empl/yed by the Elector Palatine. Settled in Haarlem, he worked with success until his death in 1693. His best works are views of towns, and sometimes landscapes, but his pictures of village merry-makings are not without merit. His works are somewhat rare in public galleries. The Berlin Museum has a *Winter Landscape,* by him—signed. He is also represented at Amsterdam, Dresden, Rotterdam, and St. Petersburg.

GERRIT BERCK-HEYDE,* the younger brother and pupil of Job,

* Or Berkheyden, or Berkeydon.

was born at Haarlem in 1638.   In 1660 he entered the Guild of St. Luke. He frequently painted in company with his brother, and they resided together with their sister Aechje. Gerrit painted at Cologne, Heidelburg, Haarlem, and Amsterdam. He died at Haarlem in 1698. He chiefly painted exteriors of Dutch buildings (Fig. 92) ; occasionally he produced a church interior, and Italian buildings. The figures of men and animals which enliven his pictures were from his own hand. His pictures are rare in public galleries. In the Amsterdam Museum we may see a view of the Cathedral, the old Town-hall, and new Church of that city. In the Louvre is a picture of Trajan's Column, showing his Italian style. In England, Berk-Heyde is occasionally found in private collections.

PIETER JANSZ SAENREDAM occupies the first place among Dutch painters of interiors. He was born at Assendelft in 1597, studied under Frans de Grebber, entered the Guild at Haarlem in 1623, and died at Haarlem in 1665. His earliest picture is a *Gothic Church* (Amsterdam Museum), dated 1636. In the Turin Gallery is *The Interior of a Protestant Church.* His masterpiece is a view of the old *Town-hall of Amsterdam,* which was burnt in 1651. The picture is in the present Town-hall.

EMANUEL DE WITTE, who was born at Alkmaar in 1607, was the scholar of Evert van Aelst, a painter of still-life at Delft. Failing as a portrait-painter, De Witte devoted himself almost entirely to the painting of interiors, choosing most frequently churches of the later Italian style. In this branch of art he is as unrivalled as Ruisdael among landscape painters. His best pictures must be sought in the Amsterdam Museum, and in the Van Loon and Van der Hoop collections of that city. An *Interior of a Church*, probably at Delft, by De Witte is in the National Gallery. De Witte painted at Delft and at Amsterdam, where he died in 1692. The influence of De Witte may be clearly seen in the works of HENDRIK VAN VLIET

FIG. 92.—VIEW OF HAARLEM. BY GERRIT BERCK-HEYDE.

(about 1605—after 1671) of Delft, and CORNELIS (?) HOEC-
GEEST, a painter of the seventeenth century, of whose life
nothing is known for certain : two interiors by him are in the
Antwerp Gallery.

Passing to the painters of still-life, we find the artists of this
class choosing various subjects, all more or less trivial; but displaying the patience, minute workmanship, harmonious colouring,
and technical truthfulness which distinguish the Dutch School
in all its branches. Sometimes the still-life represents dead
game, sometimes a meal set out—oysters, boiled lobsters, and
bread—on other occasions philosophical instruments, gold and
silver vessels, pots and pans, or a human skull, are chosen.
Nearly all the best painters of still-life also painted fruit and
flowers. Indeed, the Dutch have ever been enthusiastically fond
of flowers; and were never tired of growing them first and
painting them afterwards.

JAN DAVIDSZ DE HEEM was one of the earliest, and certainly
the best, of the painters of fruit. His arrangement, his power as
a draughtsman, and his colours, are all excellent (Fig. 93). His
two greatest pictures are to be seen in the Galleries of Berlin
and Vienna. At the latter gallery is a picture, painted in 1648,
representing the *Holy Chalice crowned with a Wreath.* Sym-
bolic sheaves of corn and bunches of grapes are mingled with
the flowers. In the Berlin Gallery (No. 963), the sides and top
and bottom of the picture consist of festoons of flowers. It
is signed JOHANNES DE HEEM, F. 1650. The picture of the
Madonna, which these flowers ornamented, was removed in 1806 ;
and is now replaced by a more modern work by Karl Begas
(1794—1854). Good work by De Heem is also seen in the
galleries of the Louvre, the Hague, Amsterdam, and Dresden.
Jan Davidsz de Heem was born at Utrecht in 1600, and studied
under his father David. He removed to Antwerp and entered
the Guild in 1636, and painted there and at Utrecht until his
death at Antwerp in 1674. CORNELIS DE HEEM (born at Utrecht

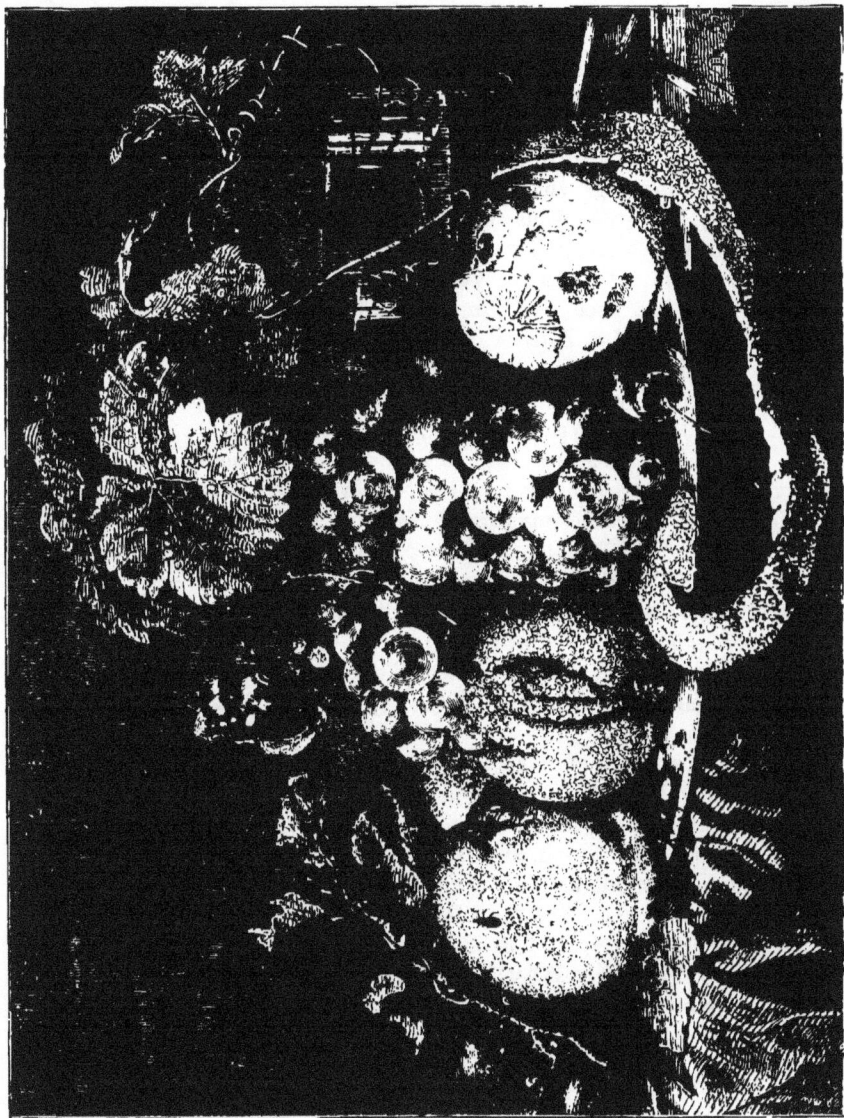

FIG. 93.—FRUIT. BY DE HEEM. *The property of M. Duclos.*

in 1623, died at the Hague after 1671), son of Jan, painted similar subjects almost as successfully.

HENDRIK MARTENSZ SORGH (not ZORGH), commonly called ROKES, was born at Rotterdam in 1621. He was a pupil of Willem Buiteweg, and is *said* to have also studied under Teniers ; his works display a knowledge of this master, and also the influence of Adriaan van Ostade and Brouwer. He died at Rotterdam in 1682. In the Van der Hoop Collection at Amsterdam there is a good *Fish-Market* by him ; and in the Louvre is an *Interior of a Kitchen ;* while in the National Gallery he is represented by *Two figures drinking,* and *Boors at Cards,* both acquired by the Henderson bequest. He is also represented in the galleries of Berlin, Dresden, and Munich.

MARIA VAN OOSTERWYCK, one of the very few female artists whom the Low Countries produced, is not so well known as she deserves to be. She was born at Nootdorp near Delft in 1630, and was a pupil of Jan Davidsz de Heem ; she found patrons in Louis XIV., William III. of England, the Emperor Leopold, and Augustus I., King of Poland. She usually painted flowers in vases, and her pictures are marvellous for their truthfulness. In the gallery of the Uffizi, Florence, and at Vienna are to be found her two best flower-pieces. She died in 1693 at Eutdam.

ABRAHAM MIGNON, who was born at Frankfort in 1639, was also a pupil of Jan Davidsz de Heem, whom he approaches when at his best. As a rule, he was much inferior to his master in arrangement, drawing, and colour. His pictures are tolerably common in public and private galleries. Mignon entered the Guild of Utrecht in 1669. He died ten years later. Another follower, if not pupil, of de Heem was—

JACOB WALSCAPELLE,* who flourished about 1670. His pictures are very rare, many of them being attributed to De Heem. A flower-piece in the Dresden Museum is thus assigned, though it

* Or Van Walskappel.

bears the signature of Walscapelle.* A picture of *Flowers, Insects, and some Strawberries*, signed JACOB WALSCAPELLE, is in the National Gallery.

RACHEL RUYSCH occupies a very prominent place among flower-painters. She sometimes painted fruit, and did so excellently. In the Hague Museum are two fine flower-pieces.

FIG. 94.—FLOWERS. BY VAN HUYSUM.

by her, both signed, one dated 1700, and the other 1715. There are also some of her best works at the Château of Wilhelmshöe, near Cassel. Rachel Ruysch was the daughter

* No. 1164 in the Dresden Gallery, "though signed with the name of Walscapelle, is there assigned to Jan D. de Heem" (Kugler's Handbook). In the official catalogue it is said to be signed "J. S. (?) D. De Heem."

of a professor of anatomy and botany. She was born at Amsterdam in 1664, studied under Willem van Aelst, and married in 1695 the portrait painter Juriaan Pool. In 1701 she entered, with her husband, the Guild of Painters at the Hague. In 1708 she was appointed Court painter to the Elector Palatine, who loaded her with presents, invited her several times to his court, and stood godfather to one of her ten children. She painted at an advanced age, and died in 1750, at Amsterdam.

JAN VAN HUYSUM, who was born at Amsterdam in 1628 began life as a scene-painter in conjunction with his father Justus and three brothers. He soon showed a marked success in flower-painting, and, devoting himself to this branch of art, achieved the highest place. He resided all his life at Amsterdam, where he died in 1749. "If De Heem, by the harmony of his warm golden colour, be called the Titian of flowers and fruits, Jan van Huysum's bright and sunny treatment entitles him to the name of the Correggio of the same branch of art" (Kugler's 'Handbook'). Van Huysum painted the details of his flowers, as the bloom and gloss on the leaves, with wonderful minuteness (Fig. 94). He sometimes attempted landscapes, but not very successfully. His flower-pieces were, and still are, highly valued. In the Louvre is a picture of flowers in a terra-cotta vase, which shows his earlier style when influenced by his work as a scene-painter. Also in the Louvre is a picture of a table spread with fruit mixed with flowers, which shows Van Huysum at his best. His pictures may likewise be found in the Amsterdam Museum, the Hague, and many other galleries; the National Gallery contains a *Vase of Flowers*, which is a masterpiece. It is signed JAN VAN HUIJSUM FECIT, 1736 EN. 1737; and in the Dulwich Gallery there are four signed works by his hand.

JAN VAN OS, who was born at Middelharnis in 1744, was a successful imitator of Van Huysum. He studied under Aart

FIG. 95.—THE FRIGHTENED FOWLS. BY D'HONDECOETER.

Schouman at the Hague, and occasionally painted landscapes, animals, and marine views; but it is as a flower-painter that he is best known. A good flower-piece by him is in the Louvre; and he is also represented by *Fruit and Flowers and Dead Birds,* signed J. VAN OS, in the National Gallery. An example of his marine pictures may be seen in the Städel Gallery at Frankfort. He died at the Hague in 1808.

Among the painters of living birds and poultry—

MELCHIOR D'HONDECOETER occupies a prominent place. He occasionally painted the grander kinds of birds, as swans and peacocks, specimens of which are in the Louvre; but the humbler denizens of the poultry-yard furnished his favourite subjects (Fig. 95). He may be seen to advantage in a *Fight between a Cock and a Turkey* (The Hermitage); *The Menagerie of Birds* (The Hague); and *The Floating Feather* (Amsterdam). In the National Gallery is a good picture by this artist, called *Domestic Poultry,* and another of *Geese and Ducks.* His works have a tendency to blackness. D'Hondecoeter, a member of a noble family of Brabant, was born at Utrecht in 1636. He first studied under his father Gijsbert, and then with his uncle J. B. Weenix. From 1659 to 1663 he is mentioned in the records of the 'Pictura' Society at the Hague. He removed to Amsterdam, where he obtained the rights of citizenship in 1688; and died in that city in 1695.

EVERT VAN AELST (born at Delft in 1602—died there in 1658), and WILLEM VAN AELST, uncle and nephew, chiefly devoted themselves to painting dead game. Willem van Aelst was born at Delft in 1620, and studied under his uncle. He spent four years in France and seven in Italy, where he was much patronized by the Grand Duke of Tuscany. From his long residence in Italy he acquired the habit of signing his works "Guilielmo (or more frequently "Guillmo") van Aelst." Van Aelst returned to Holland in 1656, and after spending some time in his native Delft, settled at Amsterdam, where he painted with great success

FIG. 96.—STILL LIFE. BY WEENIX.
In the Belvedere Gallery, Vienna.

until his death in 1679. Some of his works have been, by mistake, attributed to his uncle. His pictures are seen at Berlin, Munich, and Dresden.

JAN WEENIX, who was born at Amsterdam in 1640, was the pupil of his father, Jan Baptist Weenix. He lived for some time at Utrecht; and was also patronized by John William, Elector of the Palatinate. He died in 1719, in Amsterdam,

FIG. 97.—A KITCHEN. BY KALF.

where he had spent the greater part of his life. He chiefly painted dead animals and game, though occasionally, like his father, he attempted landscapes. His dead hares (Fig. 96) are chiefly remarkable, and sometimes rival those of Jan Fyt in marvellous minuteness of execution. Two important pictures by these two artists are in the collection of Sir Richard Wallace, and are miracles of delicate and minute finish. Many of the best pictures of Weenix are in England ; *Dead Game and Dog*, signed, and dated 1708, is in the National Gallery, and a *Shepherd clipping the hair of a Dog* is in the Dulwich Gallery.

WILLEM KALF is, *par excellence*, the painter of the kitchen. If it be a merit to be great in small matters, Kalf undoubtedly possesses that merit.   Born at Amsterdam in 1630, he studied under Hendrik Pot, and like his master painted historical subjects.   But this was not the true sphere of art for which Kalf was intended ; he commenced to paint kitchens, and if ever an artist could extract poetry from a saucepan, or beauty by the grouping of vessels on a dresser, Kalf has done so (Fig. 97).   He died in 1693 at Amsterdam.   His pictures may be seen in the Louvre, and the galleries of Dresden, Amsterdam, and Rotterdam.

Art, which was born vigorous and full of life when Holland became free, died out after the peace of Utrecht (1713), when a purely popular government was exchanged for that of hereditary Stadtholders, who quickly became kings.   The pictures of fruit, flowers, game, crockeryware and the like, however admirable in themselves, display a distinct degeneration from the vigorous works which were the fruit of the young Republic.   Those earlier pictures of the Dutch School are, like the ballads of a country, the expression of the national thought and feeling.   If an historical picture appears among them, it is a history of some national event, and intended for the Town-hall.   If a religious subject is chosen, it is meant for a sermon.   But as a rule the pictures deal with every-day life, and the painter speaks from his canvas to his brethren.   It has been observed that the

History of Painting in the Low Countries forms a parallel with
that of ancient Greece.   We have the *Divine Age*, consecrated
to religious painting by the Van Eycks and Memling; the
Heroic Age, illustrated by the chivalrous painting of Rubens
and his school; and lastly, the *Human Age*, which finds its
exponents in the burgher painters of Holland in the seventeenth
century.

FIG. 93.—VIEW OF A VILLAGE.   BY JAN FRANS VAN BREDAEL.
In the Amsterdam Gallery.

INDEX OF NAMES.

(In the arrangement of the names no notice has been taken of prefixes.)

Q

THE END.

Richard Clay & Sons, Limited, London & Bungay.

www.ingramcontent.com/pod-product-compliance
Lightning Source LLC
Chambersburg PA
CBHW020851270326
41928CB00006B/654